Destination Life Success

Destination Life Success

DESTINATION: LIFE SUCCESS

Your Map To Success in

Your Career & Your Life

DR. DEBORAH GENTRY

Written by:
Dr. Deborah Gentry

Copyright © 2021 Deborah Gentry

Gentry Development Group

www.lifesuccesschannel.com

All rights reserved. This book or parts thereof may not be reproduced in any form, stored in any retrieval system, or transmitted in any form by any means – electronic, mechanical, photocopy, recording, or otherwise – without prior written permission of the publisher, except as provided by the United States of America copyright law. For permission requests, write to the publisher, at the address below.

deborah@LifeSuccessChannel.com
Gentry Development Group
Lynchburg, Tennessee, USA

Disclaimer: This book and associated website and the content provided herein are for educational purposes. No promises are made, we provide helpful information for our readers. No liability is assumed for any losses or damages due to the information provided. You are responsible for your own actions and results.

ISBN: 978-1-7376559-0-9

Destination Life Success

To my wonderful husband, Jack, who is my editor for the book and is my forever partner in Life Success. To my children Jacqueline and Ross for being wonderful examples of real Life Success everyday.

TABLE OF CONTENTS

PART 1	1
What Is Your Life Success Destination?	1
CHAPTER 1	2
Introduction	2
CHAPTER 2	12
Getting To Your Life Success Destination	12
CHAPTER 3	22
How To Build a 5 Star Life Success Destination	22
PART TWO	31
The Five Gauges Pointing To Your	31
Life Success Destination	31
CHAPTER 4	33
The Time Gauge	33
CHAPTER 5	54
Talent Gauge	54
CHAPTER 6	94
Outlook Gauge	94
CHAPTER 7	117

Money Gauge	117
CHAPTER 8	130
Relationship Gauge	130
PART THREE	145
How To Get To Your	145
Life Success Destination	145
CHAPTER 9	146
Determine Why And Where You Want To Go	146
CHAPTER 10	169
The Road Ahead	169
Maximizing all 5 Gauges	170
A FINAL NOTE	201

PART 1

WHAT IS YOUR LIFE SUCCESS DESTINATION?

CHAPTER 1

INTRODUCTION

Are you successful? Are you happy? Are you living the life you want? The life you are meant to live?

Do you work from your own plans? Or are you dictated by other people's plans for you?

Do you have a dream? Do you have a way to get there? Or are you compromising your life's dreams?

I was a senior executive for many years in several different large global companies in charge of several hundred thousand jobs, yes, several 100,000's of people and jobs. I was ultimately responsible for their selection, hiring, training and development (along with firing unfortunately).

I've seen so many people who are not in the right jobs. And it's not their fault! Being misplaced is not good for them or for the company. *Most people are not using their best talents to achieve their full potential!* They don't feel competent with job descriptions and environments that just don't fit them and get less than stellar performance appraisals. They don't know how to build their MAP to get the the right Destination. Many would be very successful on their own if they just knew how .

My recruiters focused on finding *"qualified people"* and we would develop them for success *within the company.*

Now I have my own business helping people with their careers. I teach them how to use their talents and *where* to get their **Life Success,** which is *very different from corporate success.*

After working with thousands of people, I can tell you there are those who can achieve Life Success, and there are those who will never figure it out.

THE TALE OF 2 MEN

I met Kirk and John about the same time. (Names changed to protect identity). Both their companies hired me to coach their top staff. They were in the same industry, both multi-billion dollar organizations but two different companies.

Kirk, by all business and social standards was considered extremely successful in his role as the number two person in the company. To set an example he worked six days a week, 12 hours a day, traveled to overseas business locations two weeks a month, and was an extremely loyal employee.

He was paid well, had a nice car and a beautiful home in the country. Employees liked Kirk, that was, when he wasn't pounding them to get more production out of them. That's what his CEO demanded, and so he followed every order. Not without non-stop fights in-between, but in the end, he always did what the CEO wanted.

I worked with Kirk as his executive coach, and as a business consultant for the company for 10 years. By all business standards, he was very successful. He single-handedly made the company the most successful in their industry. I was there to help him build his team and give strategic business advice.

During that time, his marriage was constantly in trouble, he rarely saw his children, and had several serious illnesses caused by stress. I saw him face-to-face about once a week and was on the phone with him most days. He was very nice to me. But people in the company saw daily confrontations. That made him so stressed, he looked like he could pop at any moment. His peers were relentless and no matter how he tried, he couldn't make peace with any of the problem makers.

He made himself miserable. Every single day, he had face-to-face confrontations with his boss. Screaming matches. His secretary kept me up to date on daily conflicts and endless stress. She constantly worried he would have a heart attack. He had no time to himself. He would call me on his drive time almost everyday and we would go over all the problems of the day.

I knew I could not go on helping him to be "successful" at managing the business and all his people (thousands around the world). I did everything I could to try and convince him there was more to life.

It's never a good idea for an external consultant to try and get someone in their client company to leave. I would definitely be fired if they found out. I tried to get him to seriously look at other companies. His success was recognized around the globe and he would be highly valued anywhere.

Ultimately, he was incapable of understanding that to get Life Success he would have to make big changes. He just couldn't do it.

Selling Life Success in a global company was not in my list of services. Corporations couldn't care less about that. Down deep I knew that I'd have to do something different in the future to help people individually, not just for the company.

I didn't want to walk away from their business which was over $50,000 *a month* for my work. Ultimately, I moved away, and although we kept in touch, he never changed.

I became well known in Kirk's industry for my work with his company, and got another client in that industry. I was hired to coach the president of their largest division, John. He was also successful, but the company wanted me to work with him one-on-one to help boost a few areas of his business.

That assignment lasted a year or so. I'd fly down to spend a day a month with him. We'd go to his country club for lunch and get a meeting room with a white board, and we would work for hours.

John was so easy to work with. He made as much money as Kirk, but never got caught up in it. He had a great wife and kids. He only worked normal executive hours, 8 to 6. John really wanted to learn how to improve his talents and skills. Overall, he was a great and fun client.

Every single suggestion I made to help him change up something to help him on the job, he did it. And he did it right away. John never spent any time agonizing over the change. If I thought it was a good idea, he was willing to try it. (In my career as SVP of HR, I was always responsible for coaching the CEO's and all division Presidents, so I was very comfortable making business recommendations at that level).

One day a month face-to-face, a few phone calls a week, and in a year, we were done. The company was much happier, and he so was he.

No stress, no strain, no misery, no fighting with peers or bosses.

John was not known as a rollover by any means. You don't get to be President of a multi-billion dollar division that way.

John *knew what he had. He also knew what he didn't have. He knew what he wanted and was willing to get what he needed. He never hesitated to change. He loved to learn.*

Kirk was always willing to read the latest management book I recommended, but it never sank in. He had an M.B.A. and was very smart, but it didn't help. He couldn't apply any of it.

While I was working with John, I developed my 5 Gauges Model of Life Success.

- **TIME**
- **TALENTS**
- **OUTLOOK**
- **MONEY**
- **RELATIONSHIPS**

John was very smart, just like Kirk, but he didn't overpower anyone. He didn't need to. He had just as tough a boss as Kirk. However, he didn't let his boss get to him, and he still achieved his business success.

I want to compare Kirk and John for you because they basically had the exact *same job,* global responsibilities, in the *exact same industry*, but in different companies. But how different the end of the stories!

John and I worked on the 5 Gauges and he really did listen, and he really did change. We supercharged his existing Talents, and added more.

John learned how to value his Time. We spent the whole year of my coaching him on developing his Talents and Outlook. He already had a good view of Money. His Relationships which were good to start, improved along the way.

In the end, Kirk hated his work even though technically he was good at it. He harbored so much anger against the people he worked with. (Relationships) He hated going to work. He hated his boss and his peers. He agonized over all of his family relationships which never changed. He couldn't manage his Time or his Outlook. He had business success, but little Life Success. Kirk would never achieve his dreams. He did end up changing jobs into a much more manageable role for his talents in a different industry, but his overall Life Success Score didn't change much.

John, on the other hand, was willing to take a long hard look at his Talent Asset Portfolio (I will go into later), and worked my plan to achieve his own dreams and Life Success. He knew the Destination he wanted and worked hard to get there. Kirk wanted to change but ultimately was incapable of doing what it would take to get to his Life Success Destination.

So that is the Tale of 2 Men. Both had tremendous Business Success, but *only one* achieved Life Success.

WHAT IS A LIFE SUCCESS DESTINATION?

What is a Destination? Do you know where the word comes from? Late Middle English from Latin, Destinare. 'Make firm, establish'. The original sense was 'the action of **intending someone or something for a purpose**', later **'being destined for a place'**, hence the place itself. (Lexico)

Merriam Webster dictionary defines Destination:
1. **The purpose for which something is destined**
2. **An act of appointing, setting aside for a purpose**
3. **A place to which one is journeying**
4. **A place worthy of travel**

Therefore: if you choose a destination, that's where you intend to end up. A place worthy of travel.

If you *don't* choose a destination, no telling where you will end up.

It's important to have a Life Success Destination. If you don't know what it is, you surely won't get there.

> *Your Life Success Destination <u>is</u> <u>where you will be</u> when you are doing what you are meant to do in your career, or your business, and in your life. This means using your best talents <u>and</u> working in an environment that suits you best to create meaningful happiness in your life.*
> —Dr. Deborah

In my own business, I've worked with thousands of people in the course of their careers. I can tell you, there are more unhappy people than happy ones because they are not in the right job, the right career, or the right organization. This in turn affects their personal life and makes them feel like they are not successful in life overall.

I won awards for my methods on how to navigate through one's career.

Who do you know that has a fabulous personal life and a miserable job? They just don't go together.

Appearing to be successful in a job with a great salary, power and status DOES NOT translate into a happy personal life. For several reasons:

- First of all having the "Successful Job" usually means a lot of sacrifice along the way
  - Doing some work you may like, but a lot of work you don't like
  - Doing work you are not meant to do!
  - Too many hours, not enough vacation
  - Lots of organizational constraints
  - Being forced into doing things you may not agree with
  - Representing people or products you don't really believe in

Executive and entry level jobs both can have the same problems. Things definitely don't get better the higher up you get. You really don't get more control. Often you get less.

Imagine doing work that you really like to do. Work you are really good at, impactful work. Your best work will support your best personal life! Do you have that now?

- Freedom to control your time
- Time to put into a great social life, family life
- The amount of money and resources you want to support your family

Most people don't have that. *And the stress of not having those things undermines how they live every day.*

The average person works 40 hours per week, 50 weeks per year. That comes to 2,000 hours per year. Most people work 50 years, times 2,000 = 100,000 hours of work in a lifetime.

Many people work 50 hours per week (I always worked 60). That's 2500 x 50 years = 125,000 hours!

If you are going to give something 125,000 hours of your time wouldn't it be better to choose something you really want to do?

It's all about selecting the best career, the best job, the best business environment for what you want in your life. I have seen so many people crash and burn in their careers and ruin their lives. I'm committed to helping people avoid that.

DO YOU WANT MORE LIFE SUCCESS?

Is traveling to your Life Success Destination one clear path?
NO, it requires a multi-dimensional navigation system to get there. Some people figure it out, but most don't.

Life Success is *not* Life Balance. That's not what I'm talking about. Who knows what Life Balance is anyway? It changes from day to day.

You need a MAP to reach Life Success. That's what this book is meant to do. My MAP will be your guide to finding your Life Success Destination.

You might have parts of it going, but why wait for Life Success and just hope that you can get there on your own?

Your Life Success Destination will be *where you live your life to the fullest. It's where you are meant to be.*
Why don't people get to live their Life Success?
Because they don't know how!

If I said "Do you want to live your life to the fullest?" Most people would **NOT** say "No Way! Not interested!".

People don't get there because they don't have the Map. The Map to their Life Success Destination. It is definitely very hard to see your future unless you map it out. The MAP is the plan.

You and only you, are responsible for building your Life Success Destination.

If you think about your Life Success Destination like a place, it's easy to see how to get there. That's what this book is about. Helping you to be the navigator of your success and life fulfillment.

When you plan a trip you need a **Travel Agent** to get to your destination..

When you plan to get to your Life Success Destination you need a **Life Success Agent.**

Let me be your **Life Success Agent** to help you get to your Life Success Destination..I have your Map!

My Mission:

To give people the MAP they need to reach their Life Success Destination.

I want people to achieve their dreams by setting Life Success Destinations beyond where they ever thought they could go.

Once you understand you, and only you, are in charge of your life, you can start. No one else is going to make you successful. Not your boss, not your mom, not your wife, not your neighbors. Only you can do it.

ARE YOU IN A LIFE RUT?

It's so easy to get stuck in a rut. Not because you're not talented, but because your vision is limited. Can you see beyond your circumstances today? Many people focus on the demands of the day and they don't see themselves accomplishing their dreams. If you want more of the same, then keep focusing on that. What you focus on is what you're going to move toward. If you want change, get a plan! You won't get where you want to go without a plan! A Map!

The truth is, **we all have visions and dreams for our future. Every one of us has ideas of what we would like to have for our Life Success.** The question is, how can you make your vision a reality? Today, why don't you change your focus? Lift your eyes beyond your circumstances. Get a higher dream, a greater vision for your life. Let's start now.

CHAPTER 2

GETTING TO YOUR LIFE SUCCESS DESTINATION

Since 2020/2021

The way we work and the way we spend our time has changed a lot since 2020. People's jobs have changed. Many more people work from home. However that has not made things easy. In fact, it can make it more difficult in terms of finding success in both work and personal life.

FIND AN ALTERNATIVE ROUTE?

This is the time to figure out where you have come from, and where you are going to. Evaluating the things you have done and the things you still have left to do. Who you are, and who you need to become.

We've all been through difficult times. But those times have taught us somethings about ourselves.

Maybe it has made you realize you need to be innovative when faced with tough times.

I have been coaching people with completely different challenges they never faced before, since the whole concept of working and jobs changed in 2020. The way people move ahead and get promoted has changed.

All of that made having a plan for Life Success very challenging.

Do you have a plan for your life success?

If you don't have a plan for yourself, *other* people will make one for you. And what's that? **It's their plan!**

Whatever is **best for them** and their success! Not what's best for your Life Success!

Most people don't know how to change jobs or careers. All they know is they are unhappy and move along from a job at one company to the same job at another company and repeat the same problem.

- At the end of your life will you feel like you have lived the life you wanted and were supposed to live?

• Are you in control of the decisions for your day to day life and outcomes?

• Are you confident you can provide for yourself, family, and others who may need help?

• Without a job working for someone else, do you know how to make money using your talents?

Do you need help in finding your direction?

WHAT I KNOW ABOUT

LIFE SUCCESS DETOURS

I spent a lot of years getting highly educated and credentialed in my field. *But that's not the same as learning about Life Success.*

My experience in helping people is how I learned about Life Success. Coaching people in their careers while I worked in executive development/training and development for large corporations. Then having our own coaching consulting business, seeing what people are capable of achieving using sound practices and methods.

Having to deal with many ups and downs of our own lives and careers, I certainly know what it's like to have to start *over and over again* to gain our Life Success. The worst situations are when people are caught off-guard. Losing a job, losing financial security, losing a home.

Jack, my husband, and I had two devastating losses in one year. We had just built a $4,000,000, 12,000 square foot home just outside of Denver, CO. In just two months I lost my job (making $1,000,000 per year), and the two major stocks we owned from our previous companies lost $3,000,000 in our accounts. In just two months, we were broke. That money never came back. We were in a mess. We had to sell our home for half of what is was worth and even that took four years of $12,000/month house payments. We had to borrow more money to pay that. Those two events impacted us for many years and I was unemployed.

We moved back closer to Jack's family and started over with our own business. That worked well for a number of years, and then we moved again, this time to Florida. We had achieved our dream of having a home directly on the ocean.

We were able to run our business from anywhere which gave us great freedom and great life success. We had a beachfront home in Mexico Beach.

Hurricane Michael hit us, straight on at 215 m.p.h. in 2018. Our home was totally destroyed and we lost everything including our business. Our church was destroyed, our friends' homes were destroyed. It was over a hundred miles to the nearest working gas station and working power lines.

We had to move in with our daughter in Tennessee. Most of our Florida friends never recovered and many are scattered. We were lucky. So many people lost their lives in that hurricane. Far too many took their own lives after giving in to the loss and devastation. People who had businesses and lost everything saw no way forward.

How We Survived

The police forced everyone living directly on the beach to evacuate. We loaded what we could get into our two vehicles. (Many people across from the beach stayed and and many died). We drove as fast as we could right ahead of the hurricane, all the way to Tennessee.

We had my second book, *Talents From God*, finished by October 1st, 2018 and then the Michael struck. Everything was put on hold. Our home was directly on Mexico Beach when the strongest hurricane in US history (and 5th in world history), destroyed our home. Our *only* home. Not just a beach house. Our only home with all our belongings. Hurricane Michael changed our future forever.

It took six months of struggling with mortgage companies and insurance companies. None of whom deal with people like they do in their commercials. Their motivation is *not* to pay out anything. To find every way to get out of helping so *they* don't suffer financially. The state of Florida allows them to do just that so they will stay in Florida. One long exhausting fight. We're still recovering from those losses.

Our friends tell us we are the only ones who really got out as well as we did and that is because we took action immediately. We started all the calls and took action on everything that needed to be done. Most people were in shock for months. Everyone believed it would be ok. It wasn't.

I can tell you about the feeling of being homeless. It's devastating. And all of our friends were homeless as well so we had no where to go. The effects of being homeless and not having any funds to recover is absolutely frightening. Even though your home may be destroyed, the mortgage on the property still has to be paid. Every month. Utility companies were still charging us fees even without any working utilities. The lack of support from the government was shocking. FEMA inspectors were rude and never gave anyone more than a case of water. No help came from anyone except the kind people who came down on their own to the area with food.

Marshall law took effect. In a few days as soon as we were allowed in we came back but we could not move around the town without going through checkpoints. The military did their best to enforce order. We brought our RV to sleep in while we went through the rubble and all night long sirens of police went by. It was all surreal.

Being homeless was hard to believe as time went on. Even FEMA trailers didn't come in for over 6 months. People had nowhere to go. By the way, if you ever move to Florida, do NOT assume any insurance company will cover your losses. They do whatever they want to do and the state allows them to get away with it. Our monthly insurance costs were $1,000/month. And even that continued even though it was just rubble. All our neighbors had the same problem It took over a year to get any money at all from insurance and they paid as little as possible which left us in the hole for the mortgage.

Our daughter in Tennessee came down to help us dig out and to take us to her townhome. We stayed with her for four months. Three adults, two cats, three dogs in a townhome. We spent every day trying to find a place we could afford to rent. We couldn't buy anything because we still had that mortgage. Our home was completely destroyed, only two walls were still standing. FEMA said we could still live there! The floors were gone! We had to sell the lot looking like a demolition site to get the mortgage paid off. That took an act of God to get done.

Churches helped us, friends and family sent money. It's very difficult to imagine yourself not having anything. And it's definitely not something I want to do again. We were very surprised at the outreach that came from people outside of the area who drove down to bring supplies and help with cleanup. Restaurant owners from Georgia rented huge refrigerated trucks and brought down food for everyone for two months. They set up tents and cooked and served our whole town. Our gas stations were destroyed so people hauled in gas for us. These were not government people. They were people who cared from hundreds of miles away.

Almost every home was totally uninhabitable, just a pile of rubble. No electricity, no running water for a hundred miles. Everyone had to bathe in the ocean (which was not clean at that point)!

I would never have imagined how caring people can be to help those they don't know. It definitely prepared us to want to do the same for others. We are still recovering. We are being restored.

It is very challenging

TO Own Your Own Destiny

Rebuilding Life Success

WE'VE ALL EXPERIENCED A DETOUR TO LIFE SUCCESS SOMEWHERE ALONG THE WAY

Throughout the book I will tell you about many of the people we have worked with to help them achieve their Life Success Destination.

Our own Life Success story has turned out really well. We rebuilt our business and our lives. It was certainly not easy! Following our own principles we built back on our strengths, and continued our commitment to help people.

Once again we found our Life Success Destination on the water. Our home is on a gorgeous lakefront. No hurricanes! Lots of inspiration!

WHY YOU NEED A

LIFE SUCCESS DESTINATION

I had always been in the corporate world in top HR jobs, then in our own business doing executive search and consulting.

I started thinking about the hundreds of thousands of people I had managed through HR and all the rules they had to follow. My years of experience in working with people in their careers made me realize that I should summarize what I know works and what does not work for making people successful. **People really need to understand that being successful is way beyond just going to work everyday and hoping for a promotion and a raise.** There is a way for people to enjoy their work and not have to follow all the rules.

You control your Life Success Destination.

What is *your* **Life Success Destination? It's where you want to be. It's where you fulfill your life's work, your dreams, your satisfaction and your happiness.**

It's also where you are meant to be.

How do you get there?

> *If you don't know where you are going,*
> *any road will get you there.* — Lewis Carroll

My reason for doing the work I do is to make sure people get to learn the Life Success they can achieve, and how to get there. Not wandering down just any road they come to, but with the best directions to go in a straight line.

LIFE SUCCESS INSURANCE

You probably have car insurance? Home insurance? Boat insurance? RV insurance? Motorcycle insurance? Life insurance?

What we all need is Life Success Insurance. You will learn the way to **insure your own Life Success Destination** by navigating the best ways to get there.

A strong plan will withstand life's detours and accidents.

How do you get Life Success Insurance? Let me be your Life Success Agent. I'll show you how to get to where you want to go. This easy guide will lead you on a journey of discovery and accomplishment.

You need 5 stars on all your Life Success Gauges. Top off each of your gauges to get you to your Destination!

CHAPTER 3

HOW TO BUILD A 5 STAR LIFE SUCCESS DESTINATION

You have a choice on what you want your Life Success Destination to be. Where it is, what it looks like. How it feels to live there.

Will you be happy with a 1 Star Destination? (Motel 6) What would that be like? Or would you prefer to have a 5 Star Destination? (The Ritz)

Most of us want the most we can get out of life. That would be like a 5 Star Hotel. Maybe yours is a 5 Star Hotel on the beach in Maui? Or is it a small cabin in the woods out in nowhere?

Actual places are only a small part of the equation. *My definition of a Life Success Destination means fulfilling your life, wherever that may be.*

In my Life Success Destination program, you will achieve one star for mastering each of 5 Gauges of how you are doing. Five things that must be maximized to achieve your Life Success.

DO YOU FEEL LIKE YOU'RE BEING HELD BACK FROM ACHIEVING YOUR LIFE SUCCESS?

How are you doing on achieving your Life Success Destination? Arrived? Started? Don't even know what your Destination is?

Take my Life Success Destination Assessment to find out. These are the very same questions I use with my coaching clients who want to determine what is the best career, job, or business *environment* for them to maximize their Life Success. Employee? Entrepreneur? Independent?

My assessment will help you to figure out what's holding you back. It will be in your score on each gauge. So be honest. Rate yourself accurately so that you can be on your way to fulfilling your Life Success. Once you know what areas need help you can start preparing yourself to get to your Destination.

GET OUT YOUR PEN TO TAKE THE TEST AND GET READY TO WRITE OUT YOUR MAP (MASTER ACTION PLAN) IN EACH CHAPTER.

LIFE SUCCESS DESTINATION ASSESSMENT

ANSWER each question Yes or No

	TIME	Yes/No
1	I know how I want to live my life from now on	
2	I have a plan for how to prioritize my time everyday to achieve my Life Success	
3	I am given some time at work to improve myself	
4	I believe I am doing the work I am meant to do	
5	I have control over how I spend my time at work	
6	My current job is fulfilling and I am happy with the time I devote to it	
7	I have people to support me/delegate to, so I can have time to focus on what I need to be doing for my success	
8	I will be happy doing what I am doing now for the long- term	
9	I feel good about how I prioritize my time between work and my personal life.	
10	I am confident about my job security and where I will spend my future time	
	TOTAL # Yes	

	TALENT (What I'm Good At)	Yes/No
11	I know what my best talents are to reach my Life Success Destination	
12	I know how to develop my current talents	
13	I know what additional talents I need to achieve my Life Success Destination	
14	My current talents are all I need to move up to a higher level position	
15	I am confident I can change careers if I want to with the talents I have	
16	My current talents will allow me to keep my job stability if I wanted to prepare to work for myself	
17	I know how to/where to get the new talents I need to succeed	
18	I have innate talents I can use to lead me to my Life Success Destination	
19	I am maximizing the use of all of the talents I have	
20	I use talents I have to help others succeed	
	TOTAL # Yes	

	OUTLOOK (My view of my future)	Yes/No
21	I know I can achieve my Life Success Destination if I am dedicated to do it	
22	I have high expectations for myself and my future	
23	I am very happy with my job/career/business	
24	I believe there is a lot of opportunity ahead of me	
25	My career is progressing the way I want it to	
26	I am willing to take risks, even fail at times, to achieve my ultimate outcomes	
27	I have a sense of adventure	
28	I am living life on my own terms and have the independence I need to be successful	
29	I am moving forward on my journey to Life Success	
30	I really love my life as it is and I am happy	
	TOTAL # Yes	

	MONEY	Yes/No
31	I want to make a lot of money	
32	I know why I want to make a lot of money	
33	I believe being wealthy would be good for me	
34	I feel confident in my financial plan for my Life Success	
35	I already have the financial resources I need for the way I want to live in the future	
36	I understand how important money is to get to my Life Success Destination for myself, my family, and for others	
37	I know how to make money on my own	
38	I am comfortable making lots of money because I know it's good for me and to help others	
39	I am on target to make enough money to take care of myself, my family, and others	
40	I do not want to worry about money and where it will come from	
	TOTAL # Yes	

	RELATIONSHIPS	Yes/No
41	I have a strong relationship with my boss/es and know they support me and my future plans at work	
42	I have people who love and encourage me to pursue my dreams	
43	My spouse/ family support my work and future goals	
44	I am happy with my family and friend relationships	
45	I invest a lot in my relationships	
46	I am happy with my peer working relationships	
47	I have connections I can count on to help me with a new opportunity	
48	I have mentors and coaches I can count on to support my success	
49	I have strong network connections in my local and online community	
50	I can pick up the phone and call someone I don't know to ask for help with my plans	
	TOTAL # Yes	

Total how many questions you scored "Yes" for each section. Then count <u>how many of your sections</u> you scored 8 to 10 questions "Yes".

Interpreting your **LIFE SUCCESS SCORE:**

Overall I look for 80% "Yes" as a good place to be (40 out of the 50 possible points). That way you could have 4-10's and a 0 or some other combination adding up to 40. BUT it is best to have at least 80% on *each* Gauge to maximize Life Success. And that's how to get your stars!

How Many Destination Stars Do You Have Now in Your Life Success Score?

Grand Total Points	Number of Stars for Life Success Destination
All 5 Gauges 8-10 Yes	★★★★★
4 Gauges 8-10 Yes	★★★★
3 Gauges 8-10 Yes	★★★
2 Gauges 8-10 Yes	★★
1 Gauge 8-10 Yes	★
Below 8-10 Yes on all	No Stars

I built the assessment on the real questions I use with people for developing *their careers and their dreams.* These are the Gauges and the questions I know really predict Life Success. I find people are much happier when they achieve more than just job success. All the Gauges together create the environment most likely to achieve your dreams.

Now that you have your beginning Life Success Destination Score you know how many stars you've already achieved. You can work on what you want to change depending on what kind of Destination you would like to have.

I designed this assessment to be subjective. You rated yourself. You could also get someone else to take the assessment for you to see how they think you score and compare those with yours.

You'll see how many stars you have now and the areas you need to work on in order to increase your number of stars.

REMEMBER: THE MORE STARS YOU HAVE THE BETTER YOUR LIFE SUCCESS SCORE WILL BE AND THE HAPPIER YOU WILL BE

PART TWO

THE FIVE GAUGES POINTING TO YOUR

LIFE SUCCESS DESTINATION

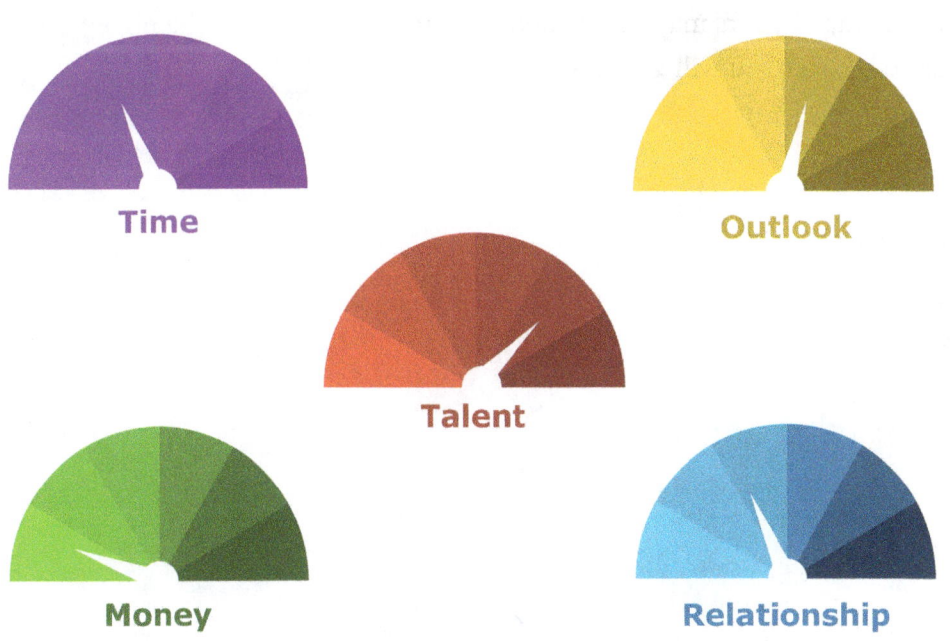

You will be focusing on the Gauges where you need to move the needle. Filling in the areas needing attention.

Each chapter in Part Two deals with one Gauge. I go through each of the ten questions for that Gauge and give my opinion on what can be done to improve. **Then I lay out more questions for each of the ten *for you* to write out what you can do** to improve on each one. YOUR ANSWERS TO THE SECOND SET OF EACH OF THE TEN QUESTIONS IS WHAT YOU WILL HAVE TO BUILD YOUR **MAP.**—THE LIFE SUCCESS **MASTER ACTION PLAN.**

The Life Success Destination Assessment measures how you're doing on the 5 Gauges. Do you have what you need to get the Highest Star Destination you want? Some of the gauges may be maxed out and ready to go. Some of yours may be low and need to be moved up. The higher they are the faster you will get there!

CHAPTER 4

THE TIME GAUGE

Your life has a set amount of time you will have on earth. Your Life Success Destination will be determined by how you spent that time.

I was the VP of Executive Development for a 30B+ conglomerate that had 130 companies with all different brands. For five years I was responsible for the top 1000 executives in the corporation across all 130 divisions all over the world.

I was responsible for making those top 1000 the most successful they could be in their business. The top 1000 is Director to President titles.

Every day I was up at 5 a.m., driving to the train station by 6, parking at the train parking lot at 6:30. Often I skated on icy roads and driving around mounds of snow in the parking lot. One hour into the city. By 7:30 I was walking 9 blocks from the train station to our building. During the winter, I literally had to hold onto ropes they put around the skyscrapers to prevent being blown away. Every winter people were killed by icicles falling from 50+ story buildings, so we kept moving!

I'd arrive at my office by 8. Being in my 42nd floor office was enjoyable because I was in a corner office with two walls of windows all the way from the ceiling to the floor, overlooking an unobstructed view of Lake Michigan.

My wonderful executive assistant and I would start the day going over my calendar and setting up our work for the day. She was highly organized and monitored who came to see me all day long.

I had meetings most of the day. Some not anticipated, like every time the CEO's secretary called and said he wanted to see me ASAP about one of our executives.

If I wasn't at the corporate office, I was on a plane going to divisions from California to New York. They always had a limo sent to my suburban home about 5 a.m. to take me to the airport to pick me up. Door to door. I worked in the limo, worked on the planes. Usually I didn't want to stay overnight, so wherever I traveled I did a one day turnaround which was intense. The limo would deliver me back home about 11 at night.

Many professional organizations asked me to present. I was regularly invited to present my model of Executive Development to other companies across the country. I became so well known for my model, I was asked to compete at Harvard Business School in front of the faculty and business heads. (And I won).

I only tell you this to paint the picture: I certainly was NOT the model of personal time management.

I did whatever it took to make everyone else successful. I was very good at it. (And I was pretty successful too). But I missed a lot at home.

I did have the weekends for my family. But I could only survive raising two children by having a full-time nanny and a full-time housekeeper to take care of our large home.

It's funny because one of the things I did was to write a book for the CEO/Chairman of the Board about priorities. With his name on it (but I wrote the whole thing as I did all of his communications and speeches to all the presidents).

It was called *The Priorities of Management*. Of course, all of the priorities were for the company. All 1000 people got a copy for required reading.

I had convinced the CEO that all executives needed to be trained on how to think like an entrepreneur. To run the business as if it was their own. A big part of the book was the motivation to think like entrepreneurs (our CEO had been an entrepreneur when he started the company, later his company became part of the conglomerate and he was CEO of it). The other priorities had to do with financial goals and leadership.

During all my corporate years, that was my focus. Helping people to make the big organization successful. I had to develop them into *what the company needed. Nothing on what the executives* needed for their own Life Success.

PRIORITIES OF MANAGEMENT (POM)

VS

PRIORITIES OF MINE (POM)

Everyone referred to my book (well, the book I wrote for the CEO), as POM. And it was focused on how each executive could contribute the most to the company.

Now I have a different POM: Priorities of Mine!!!

In my next assignment I took a job to be SVP of Human Resources again for a very large company. Well that, was a 7 day-a-week job which never panned out long term. Not a minute without an executive calling me. And quickly after I got there, we laid off 65,000 people. What a nightmare! No time at all with my family.

I landed a SVP HR job out West, a big move for our family. My Time only got worse. Executives on my doorstep all hours of the day. On the phone 24-7. We had locations in several countries. I commuted an hour downtown each way, worked 12 to 14 hours a day, 7 days a week with a relentless, narcissistic CEO. One night, coming home late, I'll never forget our daughter saying "Mom, do you realize you have not had dinner with us in over two years?" Well, that surely hit home. She was right!

I still had the nannies and the housekeeper so the children and the house were taken care of and my husband got meals and clean clothes. But my schedule and travel surely didn't lead to Life Success.

Then we built the 12,000 S.F. home in the mountains that ended in disaster. Not Life Success!!

Just so you know, the end of the story is that our two kids both became doctors, and they had a great childhood. My husband, Jack worked from home and spent a lot of the day with them. The nanny and housekeeper kept everything running well.

Over the years I learned how important it is to have my POM's straight to get our Life Success. Now I have almost total control over my Time.

Look at your calendar for the next week. What do you like that you have booked? What don't you like? If it looks like there are more things you don't like (even hate) to do, you need to assess your time.

THE ASSESSMENT QUESTIONS FOR TIME:

1. I know how I want to live my life from now on

This question inevitably involves how you want to spend the time you have left in your life. It's a very big question. I could write a whole book just on this alone.

How you spend your Time *IS* your life. Your life *IS* your Time.

From a Life Success perspective it is *how well* you spend that time. What are you doing right this minute? Reading this book! Is that a good use of your time to build your Life Success? I certainly think so. Any time you use to make things better for yourself or for others is time well spent.

The second meaning of the question is Do You Know What You Want to Do With the Rest of Your Life? That's a REALLY BIG question. In coaching, I can spend several sessions with a client just helping them to figure out this one.

Ultimately you have to decide the best use of your time everyday and is that getting you to where you want to be? Your Life Success Destination?

Obviously not every minute of every day can be used for that. There are daily chores, and helping others. But in the midst of all that, there is plenty of time to think. That's what I do.

I don't waste time sitting at a stop light. I shouldn't admit this, but I keep a notebook and pen in the passenger seat and at stoplights I'll make a note to myself about something I want to write, or an idea for someone to use or to help someone I'm coaching.

Drive time is often my best thinking time. We now live just 90 minutes from our kids, and it's a beautiful country road trip. No traffic. So I always plan on thinking about something I need to work out, or to write, or think about my own Life Success plan along the way.

2. I have a plan for how to prioritize my time everyday to achieve my Life Success

3. I am given some time at work to improve myself

Two big Time topics for people in coaching with me are Questions 2 and 3. I also wrote a companion book to this one called: The Life Success Action Plan which comes with my coaching program to implement your MAP (MASTER ACTION PLAN) to reach your Destination.

START YOUR ENGINE WITH AN ACTION PLAN

One of my favorite sayings is: **Fail to Plan, Plan to Fail.** I've learned the hard way, you can't plan everything, but planning nothing is way worse.

Kirk, my first story, let his secretary book meetings for him, but he never ran on time and never scheduled time for actual work. Everyday a tsunami would walk through the door, or a call from overseas, with something big. Of course, Kirk would have to stop everything and attend to it. The problem was, everything was an emergency. He never wanted to delegate problems. He had to solve each one himself. Better planning, scheduling and delegating would have helped a lot, but he couldn't let go.

If you are an employee or if you are your own boss, trust me, planning is critical. If you work at home, planning is critical.

You are very unlikely to achieve your Life Success Destination without careful time planning.

I think I've probably taken every time management course there ever was. I've tried the priorities methods, the A,B,C's, all the stars, the different color markers, different pages for tasks, goals, and on and on, including paper and digital planners.

Planners are not going to get you where you want to go. *You'll spend so much time filling out the pages you won't have time to get anything else done.*

That kind of Time planning is not what I'm talking about. I'm talking about planning your time for Life Success, not planning lunch dates, your workouts, or time for grocery shopping. Plan how you will achieve your Life Success Destination one day at a time.

My Life Success Action Plan focuses on just a few things a day and each is well thought out in reverse. Starting at the end (the Destination) and planning backwards day by day.

How did you rate yourself on those two questions? You probably have a really good idea of how you're doing on Time planning.

Having a plan and executing a plan are two different things. It depends on whether or not you have control over your time.

Letting the tsunami roll through your door everyday is not the way to manage your time. You can't make any progress living from emergency to emergency. You need to leave some open time slots to deal with those.

That leads us to question 3: I am given time **at work** to improve myself. I'm not talking about doing crossword puzzles or putting together the shopping list, or making personal phone calls.

I'm talking about using your time at work for professional development, learning new skills. This is difficult for people working in companies where they have specific tasks that have to be done hour by hour.

In my organizations where I was head of HR or head of Executive Training and Development, we dedicated time for people to learn new skills, often assigning them specific projects where they would learn those. All my succession plans for people were based on what they needed to learn to prepare for their next promotion. Often I would have them work with someone who already had that job or cross-training.

It's a really good idea to ask what your future jobs look like and what training are you going to receive to prepare you for that. The more specific Professional Development Plan you can get, the better.

I used to make 6 month plans for every person considered to be a "High Potential". Even if I didn't know exactly where they were going they had a development plan.

Most organizations today do the opposite. First of all, Performance Appraisals have become the way to limit raises, or any change to compensation. For that reason, Performance Appraisals have become more focused on what people can't do (often referred to as Performance Improvement needs). Ever had a PIP? A Performance Improvement Plan? That means you have one foot out the door. Start looking for another job. Again, always focused on what the organization needs, RARELY on what the individual needs or to strengthen talents they already have.

I believe the way to maximize people's performance is to create jobs based on what people's talents are, rather than squeezing them into jobs strictly based on what the organization needs. When you do that, there are a lot of poor fits, leading to poor performance. They like to concentrate on what you can't do (known as performance development needs) rather than on what you can do. Organizations spend way too much time trying to get people to do things they just aren't good at and then punish them for that. I believe people should be groomed for talents they have. Take those talents to higher levels and don't waste so much time on things they may never master.

Every person is different. Squeezing them into cookie cutter boxes just doesn't work for the organization or the individual. Most companies base job titles on a compensation structure so all people in the same title are in the same pay range. I believe using pay as the main factor causes this situation. Job titles are then chained to specific job descriptions. The whole system is designed for the organization, not for any individual's benefit. I should know, I had to design and implement them. There is a much better way to do this which would benefit individuals *and* organizations.

I think organizations who allow people more freedom to contribute are the most successful ones.

4. I believe I am doing the work I am meant to do

If you scored yourself high on this one, you are on the right track to your Destination. If you are using your best talents (more on that later) and applying them to the right work, you should feel very good. If you don't, the big question is why not?

This is a TIME question. Doing the work you are meant to do means **focusing your time on doing that work.**

Or maybe you don't know what that work is. Are you spending time trying to figure that out?

Maybe you are held back from getting there. Or maybe someone is holding you back. Often responsibilities get put in first place during times we would like to be focused on getting to where we really think we should be.

I can tell you from the experience of working with so many people, once you know what that work is, getting there will be a positive experience. Unlike like pushing yourself, working a job that you are not meant to do. That's self-defeating and will wear you out so you don't have the time you need to get to your best work.

AN UNFULFILLED LIFE

Sarah is a very successful lawyer, by all outside accounts. In the mid-size midwest city she lives in, she can't go anywhere without being recognized. She is on boards, makes a big income, has a big practice with lots of employees. But she knows she is missing something big.

She keeps herself in great shape, buys gorgeous clothes, and is a very thoughtful person, always willing to help anyone who needs her help. I met her at a party and the first time I saw her I immediately kept watching her because she was the focal point of the room. Vivacious, beautiful, well-spoken, confident.

I've known Sarah for several years. She asks for my help every few months. But she never has Time to actually start into a program. Nearly every time we speak, she talks about how unhappy she is. She really does not like her work, or her law practice, and she really wants to do something else, but she doesn't know what. She works very very hard, six days a week, and is never happy with her work.

Her exterior shows one person. Her interior is a different one. Outwardly she looks like she has it all. A package of having it all right. She doesn't.

She has grown children all in their early 20's. Her husband stayed home to raise their four kids while Sarah worked hard to build her practice. In addition to being really unhappy with her work, I read in-between the lines her sadness because the children have not been able to gain any solid footing. None graduated from college. None have a good paying job or a good relationship with a potential spouse.

She wasn't home, so she didn't feel like she had a right to complain. But her husband, a complete opposite personality, let the kids do whatever they wanted. She spent $50,000 per year, per child in private schools. I think he expected the schools to do his work. They didn't. I'm quite sure she suffers regret in not being there to guide them more.

Still in her 50's she is completely off track for real Life Success. If she stays on the same track she is on, she will not find her Life Success

Destination. She has tried taking on lots of new things in her practice to be even more successful, but none have panned out.

She is focused on finding her "Life Purpose" and she thinks that when she finds it, then she will be fine. So she says. She thinks that means starting an orphanage, or starting a community program for needy people. Unfortunately, she has not figured out what that is even though she's spent years looking for it.

She could do all of that, and still not achieve her Life Success.

We don't teach "Finding Your Life Purpose" because we think just having one big thing to figure out is too much. Most people won't find it. She has been looking for hers for years, and still has no idea what it is.

I do know that **when you are doing the work you were meant to do you will know it and it will be fulfilling.** *And the Time* you spend on it will be positive. Using your Time the way you need to find your Destination is very, very important! You don't want to look back with regret.

5. I have control over how I spend my time at work

This is different from being able to prioritize.

If you work for a large organization you probably have very little control over your time. Even if you are an officer, your time is not your own. I have been a corporate officer and I had very little control over my time during the day. Which of course meant I had to get in really early and stay really late to get things done. There is an understanding that 8 to 5 is for meetings and before 8 and after 5 is for doing your own work. That is just work for the company.

I spent more time than I can count doing my homework alongside the kids doing theirs.

6. My current job is fulfilling and I am happy with the time I devote to it

A lower rating on this question is a predictor of job satisfaction for the future. If you don't think you are progressing in your current job, in your organization, it's likely you're not going anywhere.

If you don't start making choices on how to spend your time, your career will end up at a Destination where you don't want to be.

Your choice is to push for job progression there or to seek a new opportunity.

Remember it might be that you're not ready for the next move you want to have. Ask for a Professional Development Plan from your organization. That used to be the most common way for companies to prepare people for future job advancement. Organizations just use a Performance Appraisal with an attached Performance Improvement Plan which has a whole different connotation. Completely tied to the Compensation Plan. And the pools for raises are divided up in such a way that only some can get raises. Appraisals are used to justify who gets a raise and who doesn't, which makes sense except that a lot of people have to be rated lower than they should be because the organization can't give raises to all.

In my companies I always fought for people who needed the opportunity to advance. It's not fair to tie it all together.

It's also the vehicle used first in deciding who stays and who goes in a layoff. The pressure for results is very high.

If your career is progressing the way you want it, good for you! If you are not employed by others, are an entrepreneur or just work for yourself, you have control of that.

Working hard in a situation where you see a good future makes it feel like you're investing your TIME well.

7. I have people to support me/delegate to, so I can have time to focus on what I need to be doing for my success

If you have this in a job working for someone else, consider yourself fortunate. In my last couple of jobs I delegated to my staffs of over 300 people. And I had high level Executive Assistants who could take on actual parts of my job. Few people have that luxury. When people report to you, they basically have to take on anything you need them to do. The downside of that is managing all those people and the people to whom they provided services.

This question also can apply to having people at home/outside of work, to help you. That helps you protect your time to do the things you need to do for yourself, and gives you a leg up on getting to your Life Success Destination.

8. I will be happy doing the work I am doing now for the long term

The reason for this question is there's a big difference for people who can do something for a short time, versus realizing it could be their career for the long term. For instance, working a job while going to school. Working a job while waiting for something else to happen in your life. People do a lot of temporary things to make a living. Will you be happy doing that for the long term?

I was in the dentist's office a few days ago and I could clearly hear a patient talking to his hygienist in the cubical next to mine. He was telling her that he had been living in that small town for 25 years. "I came to visit because my wife had a family member here. We decided to stay for a little while so I got a job. Year after year went by. I'm still in that same job. Never changed. Never moved out of town. Stayed in the same house, same job for 25 years. I never planned it that way."

What you had to hear was the regretful tone in his voice. I wanted to jump up and go next door to tell him "Your life is not over, you are not committed to having to stay in that job or this town for the rest of your life. Get up and do something!" But I didn't. He's right; he never planned and so therefore he's still living the same life, year after year. And very unhappy. He'll never know what he could be doing. Just because he never had a clue about where he really wanted to go. He had no Life Success Destination.

Unfortunately, so many start off in a job because they can't find what they really want to do and then week by week, month by month, year by year **it becomes their career by default.** "Groundhog Day."

How you feel about your work is a big indicator of your progress toward your Destination.

9. I feel good about how I prioritize my time between work and my personal life

TIME has so many components of overall Life Success and how you allocate it between your work and your non-work is critical. Of course there are times when you have to sacrifice to devote your TIME to something that absolutely must get done. Doing that for the long term is not good for your personal life or health.

Showing you are the hardest worker on the team has its shortfalls. First of all you are setting a precedent which will be hard to break. People (in particular bosses) will start to expect that all the time. And it's an easy trap to put yourself into.

In the whole plan for your Life Success you definitely need to do a good job on this one.

10. I am confident about my job security and where I will spend my future time

This is another really big question. You won't be surprised to find out most people score this one low. For sure, confidence in job security for the near future is shaky for those who are employed. The average person only has a three year tenure with any one employer.

And that is a key TIME gauge. How long do you have security? How can you plan that? What can you do about it?

ACTION STEPS I WILL TAKE TO INCREASE MY SCORE ON THE TIME GAUGE:

Looking at your answers for questions 1 through 10, what can you do to get a full star on this gauge?

Write in the blank areas how you think you are doing on this and what you can improve on to get moving toward your Destination. THESE ANSWERS WILL FORM YOUR MAP (MASTER ACTION PLAN) TO YOUR LIFE SUCCESS DESTINATION!

1. I know how I want to live my life from now on

Write down your ideal way to spend each day as well as your dreams for the future.

2. I have a plan for how to prioritize my time everyday to achieve my Life Success

What is your plan? What will you do differently?

3. I am given some time at work to improve myself

If you are employed, you your time belongs to your employer. However there are many ways to ask for assignments or training that will grow your talents. What can you do?

4. I believe I am doing the work I am meant to do

What work? Be specific.

5. I have control over how I spend my time at work

If you don't, how can you change that? Or, is it time for a change to a new position?

6. My current job is fulfilling and I am happy with the time I devote to it

Most people who are employed want things to be better than they are. What can you do?

7. **I have people to support me/delegate to, so I can have time to focus on what I need to be doing for my success**

If not, how can you get support? You can ask for it.

8. **I will be happy doing the work I am doing now for the long term.**

If you are, great. You are lucky! If not, what do you think you should do?

9. **I feel good about how I prioritize my time between work and my personal life**

Often this is easier in a predictable job with a predictable schedule, and predictable work flow. If you're not in that situation, or if you have a lot of overtime, what can you do to change this? You only get one go-around with a family/partners and you don't want to alienate them. They need your time and attention. However you can share your plans with them to let them know what you are doing is temporary while you get to your Life Success Destination. What can you do?

10. I am confident about my job security and where I will spend my future time

What do you think?

CHAPTER 5

TALENT GAUGE

Are you more concerned about

WHO YOU WANT TO BE?

OR

WHAT YOU WANT TO DO?

Your answer **will determine your future Life Success Destination.**

Most people are influenced growing up being asked the BE question: "What (who) do you want to BE when you grow up?" Kids commonly answer a policeman, a teacher, a nurse, a doctor…or this generation more likely "a superhero".

Did anyone ever ask you "What do you want to DO when you grow up?"

It's a very different question. And requires very different talents. If you wanted to be an accountant you went to school to study accounting. To be a lawyer you have to study law.

For example, a large percentage of the lawyers and accountants we meet really don't like "What They DO" every day. They just liked the idea of being a lawyer.

That's the difference and people don't think about that when choosing a career. "What am I actually going to DO in my job, day-to-day?" Studying the law, studying accounting has nothing to do with the practice of law or accounting.

The number one complaint I hear from attorneys is that they didn't realize how much conflict is involved in their jobs. So while they thought that being a lawyer was a prestigious job, what they didn't know is that DOING that job requires talents they don't teach in law school, like how to deal with conflict. How to deal with angry people, clients, and all the people involved in a case, or in a contract every day. Lots of stress to deal with, because that's what they DO. I have transitioned many lawyers into different careers and they are much happier.

Same thing for accountants (and I can name many other jobs, particularly in Information Technology, IT) that realize that too late, accounting is not that much fun. Dealing with numbers and spreadsheets can be boring. You don't get to spend most of your day with people (if you like spending time with people).

It really is important for you to think about what you really want to DO rather than focusing on a job title (who/what you want to BE). A title is always temporary.

I am guilty of having spent a whole lot of years working just to attain a title I really wanted: Senior Vice President of Human Resources. Previous bosses who had that job warned me ,"You don't want that brass ring. It's nothing but trouble." They were right. In the large global companies I helped lead, I had to deal with all the officers (I was one of them) and all the board of director members.

I was much happier being a Vice President of Executive Development where what I did (DO) was help people develop into their success. The SVP HR (me) deals with all the problems people have in the whole organization. Keeping the CEO and all the other officers happy was a nightmare. I was much happier simply DOING what I love which is helping other people gain their own success.

Another reason people go for the title and power is money. I made over half a million dollars a year in the SVP jobs, but was way happier in the jobs making less than half that as head of Executive Development.

Understanding what talents you have, and how you can acquire new ones, will lead you to WHAT YOU WANT TO DO in your Life Success Destination. Job titles are not important to your long-term success and happiness. DOING what you're good at is more important.

So let's look at the talents you have to start with.

THE ASSESSMENT QUESTIONS FOR TALENTS:

11. I know what my best talents are to reach my Life Success Destination

Most people have a general sense of their talents, but a lot don't. My book called "Talents From God" has a lot of great ideas on how to figure out what your talents are.

Go through the checklist below. My Talent Asset Portfolio (TAP) will give you a good start on how you rate your own talents.

These are not job responsibilities. They are knowledge and abilities needed to succeed in different jobs.

Talent Asset Portfolio™

For Life Success

A list to get you thinking about your talents is below. Rate yours High, Medium or Low in terms of how developed you think each of your talents are <u>now</u>.

TAP WORK TALENTS	High ✓	Average ✓	Low ✓
Achieve Personal Goals			
Achieve Goals Set for Me			
Administrative/Office			
Adaptability			
Analytical			
Anticipative			
Articulate			
Artistic			
Assertiveness			
Attract Others			
Build			
Collaborate			
Communication Verbal			

TAP WORK TALENTS	High ✓	Average ✓	Low ✓
Communication Written			
Cultivate a Broad Network			
Creativity			
Credibility			
Critical Thinking			
Coaching			
Collaborate			
Confidence			
Conflict Management			
Coordinate			
Courage			
Counseling			
Curiosity			
Decisiveness /Know How to Make Good Decisions			
Delegating			
Deliver What I Promise			
Designing			
Determination			

TAP WORK TALENTS

	High ✓	Average ✓	Low ✓
Discipline			
Drive			
Encouraging			
Energy			
Entrepreneurship			
Financial			
Flexibility			
Get Things Done			
Happy			
Humor			
Imagination			
Independence			
Influencing			
Innovative			
Insightful			
Intelligent			
Judgement			
Know How to Make Money on Own			
Know How to Make Money for Others			

TAP WORK TALENTS

	High	Average	Low
Leading Others Toward a Goal			
Learning New Complex Information			
Listening			
Logic			
Mathematical			
Mechanical			
Motivating			
Memory			
Musical			
Negotiate			
Operate Equipment			
Optimism			
Organizing			
Outgoing			
People Relationships			
People Management			
Performing in Public			
Perspective			
Perseverance			

TAP WORK TALENTS

	High ✓	Average ✓	Low ✓
Persuasiveness			
Presenting/Public Speaking			
Pursuing New Opportunities			
Planning			
Prioritization			
Productive			
Problem Analysis			
Project Management			
Repair Things			
Results Oriented			
Risk-taking			
Scientific			
Service			
Sell Ideas			
Sell Products			
Set Ambitious Targets			
Social			
Strategic			
Tactical			

TAP WORK TALENTS	High ✓	Average ✓	Low ✓
Teaching			
Technological			
Thinking			
Trustworthy			
Time Management			
Vision			
Voice			

NOTE: Add any of your own talents you don't see on the list. In addition to this list is a long list of Physical Talents that can also apply to work.

How do you start your portfolio? By thinking through what talents you use, and those you have that you don't use.

This is NOT a performance appraisal or a resume, because those are only things an organization wants from you. You have a lot more than that. Think beyond your current job to identify your talents.

What did you learn about your TAP?

Go back and highlight all the talents you scored High on. Usually the ones we think we are the best at are the ones we are most proud of and have helped us the most in life. If you want someone else's opinion, ask those you know you well to rate your talents for you to compare.

Love what you are good at !!!

Take your strongest talents to work!

MY TOP 5 TALENTS ARE:

1.

2.

3.

4.

5.

What do you think about that list?

What jobs, what kind of work do you think those match up with best?

These are the talents you can focus on developing for the future. Most companies evaluate their employees on the talents that are most important to the job. Then they come up with a performance improvement plan, or a development plan, to improve those.

What always amazed me is how often this does not work out for the best for either party. Why jam people into jobs they're not well-suited for and try to get them there? You may have experienced this.

Also, think about how it feels to have your boss tell you all the things you aren't good at?

Wouldn't it be a lot better to know what you are good at and to work with those talents and continue to improve on the things you already have a talent for?

I'm not saying to ignore what you're not as good at, but why go from job to job feeling incompetent in some areas that just don't matter to you?

If you have to have a particular competency to get a particular job you really want, you will have to acquire that skill. I'm talking about the *bigger picture* of building a career based on what you're naturally good at.

In other words, don't take jobs you know have requirements you will have a difficult time with, or don't like to do. You will never be happy.

This sounds like a no-brainer, but trust me, people don't look for jobs based on that. They are attracted to *titles, power, influence, and most of all, money.* Either the person wants it for themselves, or to impress their family, friends and co-workers. Competition at work is a powerful thing. A game very few are good at. I could spend hours telling stories of people I worked with who ruined the careers of people all around them, just to get the job they wanted for themselves. Those I disliked the most were the ones who made others look bad in order to make themselves look good. They would literally step on people just to move ahead.

In all the companies where I headed up HR I started programs to assess people's talents and to select people into jobs based on those talents. Assessment and Selection — the most important processes a company can do to be a successful organization.

So look again at your TAP work talents. Now take a good look at the column of talents you score low on. Are those things you struggle with in your current job? If not, don't worry about them.

What kinds of work/careers do you think would be best for you using the first two columns of your TAP?

Many people suffer from not getting to do the work they really were meant to do. **When you get to do what you are best at, you are much happier and successful.** Most don't know what work they should do. And they don't know all of their alternatives. Many people just get stuck using only a select group of talents even though they could use more.

EXAMPLE:

Take for example Brenda who was a logistics professional. She came to my office and asked me for help. She was not a paid client, but a friend of mine asked me to see her because she had been unemployed for over two years. A single mother, she was desperate to find a job. She came to my office. Her unemployment had run out. I asked her to bring her resume.

We talked for a long time. I asked Brenda what kind of job she was looking for. She said she only wanted "her job" which meant a very specific logistics job. She made good money doing that job.

I said, "Brenda, are there any jobs like that open?" "No, she said. I'm hoping there will be soon.".

"Are you willing to move?"

"No."

I said, "How are you supporting your kids?" (She was divorced and not getting any support).

She said it was very tough. My friend had told me Brenda was desperate. I looked at her resume and talked to her about other talents she had.

I said, "Brenda, you could do other work, such as sales. You have other strong talents." Brenda said, "No, I don't want to do that." I told her I could get her a sales job tomorrow. She turned it down. I asked why not? "Because I am waiting for MY JOB to come open" she said.

What Brenda meant was she wanted her exact same job for another company to come open and she was going to wait for that.

She looked for two years. She came to me hoping I would find that one job for her. It was not going to happen. She could not see her skills getting her different job. I could have gotten her many different jobs. She used to make a good salary. But then she went to 0. She had lots of other talents qualified for many other jobs.

Brenda was one of the saddest people I ever coached (she never was a real client I was just trying to counsel her one time). She just would not listen. And I was willing to do it for free! She just could not do it. I don't think she ever did get job. I don't know what happened to her and her children. She just couldn't see another path.

12 I know how to develop my current talents

You can't assume your employer will help you with your personal/professional development. Do NOT leave this up to others. **IT'S TOO IMPORTANT TO YOUR LIFE SUCCESS!** You have to take matters into your own hands. Those that do get it done.

I guarantee you it works and even my best President level coaching clients who did that ended up way more successful. Ask people to help you develop what you need if you need help. If you don't ask, it won't happen.

13. I know what additional talents I need to achieve my Life Success Destination

Do you? If so, you would be the rare one. Most people have no idea.

Especially if you don't know your Destination, you can't know what you need to get there.

Richard is a good example: His employer, a large organization, moved everyone home to work during COVID. Then working from home became iffy and he was afraid he was going to lose his job. He has been in very specialized IT roles for over 20 years. " Maybe they will not need what I do anymore," he thought.

Week after week, Richard became increasingly concerned that he would lose his job. He has a wife and 3 girls to support.

Richard's worry turned to depression. His doctor recommended he give me a call to help.

He knows his experience is so unique, working on a particular software program used only in a particular industry.

There is only one company in his city that uses it. Nowhere to pivot to there. He's a captive to that company. He knows that if he loses that job, he has nowhere to go, he will have to uproot his family.

I helped Richard realize he may not be in the job he's meant to do for his Life Success. He believed he could only do "His Job" that he had done for 20 years, he never thought about a different job, or career.

This is soooo common. People become their job.

We worked intensively together to help him identify all his talents.

We assessed those talents, and his experience, and I showed him he can apply a lot of that knowledge to many different careers.

Now he sees he has a wide range of possibilities.

No finding the same job in another organization and staying in town. He must change if he wants to stay there.

Using our Life Success Action Plan Richard worked with me to design a plan to add to the talents he has.

We developed his plan to renovate his talents. Even though he technically is in IT, his day-to-day responsibilities really are heavily based on providing extensive customer service to the organization. He had no idea that many of his talents and responsibilities are exactly what is used in customer service management jobs. I can see it so easily because I've been responsible for jobs from the bottom to the top of multiple companies each with over 100,000 people.

I helped him dissect his responsibilities so he could emphasize those customer service pieces he really hadn't thought about before.

I also recommended a customer service course for managers to understand the process. He had the basic talents and he had the responsibility, but taking additional programs/certifications would help a lot in a job search.

He was ready to have me help him reposition his resume and re-write his job search.

I helped him to re-start. Now he is confidently looking for new jobs while he waits to hear on his current one. He knows there are many jobs he can do with his current level of compensation.

Richard is so excited about his new career possibilities, he's going to apply for those jobs in his current town. Turns out, he says he really didn't like IT now that he knows he has options in other careers.

The customer service management jobs fit his overall talents and personality better.

Helping people change in this time requires a lot of coaxing to reposition how they see themselves. The most important thing is to help them face reality and realize what all they can do. I show them that their TALENTS ARE TRANSFERABLE to different careers.

I teach people how to make a plan for their Life Success Destination. Once they have a plan to succeed, they are excited to move forward. I'M SURE YOU ALSO HAVE SO MUCH MORE YOU COULD DO! JUST BE OPEN MINDED AND MAP IT OUT.

14. My current talents are all I need to move up to a higher level position

Do you ever feel like you've been dealt the perfect winning poker hand? One that will beat anything else?

That's one way of looking at how you feel when you are on the winning track to your Destination. Are you known for specific talents? If not, you need to let other people see them/know about them. Modesty is not the road to your Life Success Destination! Don't keep them a secret! PLAY YOUR HAND!

Are you doing the work you thought you would do earlier in your career, or when you got out of school? Most people are not. People don't realize the impact of taking their first job and how that often drives their career path even if it's not what they intended to do.

Often we take jobs based on location or a good offer. They may or may not pan out the way we expected. **If you're not satisfied with what you are doing it's probably because you're not on the right road to your Life Success Destination. If you don't really feel successful, you're not.**

This may sound selfish, but the one person you need to focus on is yourself. It's like the airplane rule: "Put on your own oxygen mask first" so you can help others. It's the only way.

If you spend all your time focusing on what other people need, not only will you not be successful, but you will not be able to help them.

15. I am confident I can change careers if I want to with the talents I have

How do you score on this question? Changing careers is the hardest thing people can attempt to do on their own.

Maybe you're not happy with the career you have.

Maybe you've already tried to get the job in the new career you really want with the talents and experience you currently have. You know it's hard to do. It's not just having the right talents, it's also having the right level of developed talents.

If you have even some of the talent, it's good because you can start there and develop those further.

Matching up your current talents with what you need for the ideal situation takes some significant self-assessment and forward thinking to put it all together.

If you are an employee, it's unlikely your employer will give you any development to prepare you for a different career outside of their organization. It's really difficult to get changes outside of your function to a new career (like from a finance job to a marketing job). They will only help you develop your talents in your current function (example from a financial analyst to a financial manager) and only then if it's in their best interest.

EXAMPLE TAP COMPARISON

I have a short example of how to evaluate the talents you have to match up to a job you want to explore.

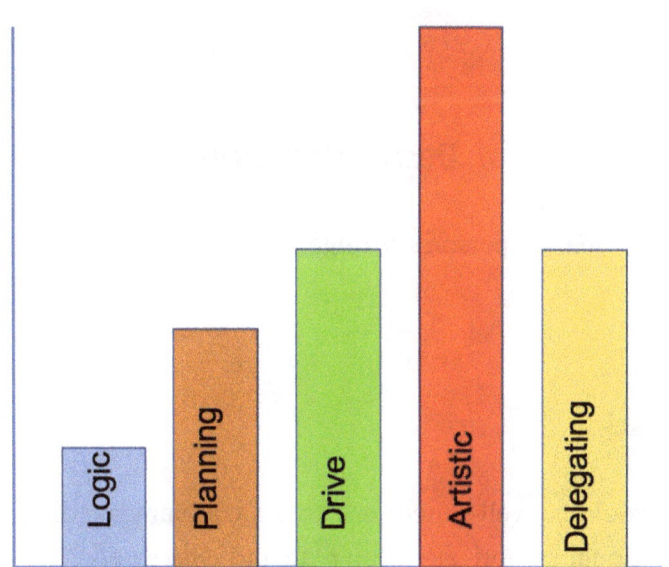

My Current Talents

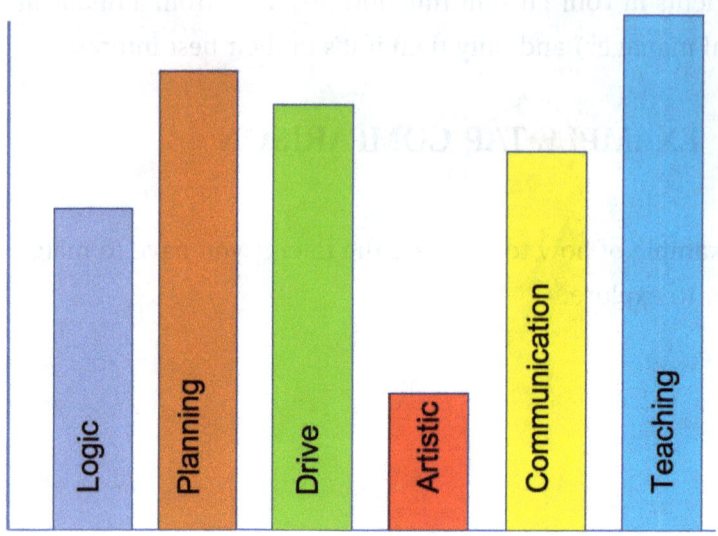

Talents Needed for Destination Job

In the first chart you can see the person's strongest talents are
1. Artistic
2. Drive
3. Delegating
4. Planning
5. Logic

Their current talents would be well-suited for either a company needing someone very creative, reasonable motivated, can plan and who can delegate some work. Perhaps a job in advertising focusing most on the creative part.

But what if that person really wants a job as a trainer? Maybe in a company, or in a school environment.

The requirements are much different. Although the person has many of the talents required, they are not at the right levels. There are also two talents they don't have at all. Communication and Teaching and they are needed at a significant level of development.

What to do? If you want to change careers you may have to develop talents you have to a higher degree *and* you will definitely have to develop new talents you haven't used before.

This is a hard sell to a business. It's even a hard sell in a not-for-profit organization. If you want to do this as your own venture, you can do whatever you want if you are willing to develop the talents you need.

16. My current talents will allow me to keep my job stability if I want to prepare to work for myself

This takes the last question to another step which is the decision to try and move toward your ideal career within an organization or to go out on your own. If you truly want to do something else, you need a plan to move forward. You can keep the job you have to support you developing the talents you need to go out on your own. You'll have a steady income while you are acquiring what else you need to move ahead to your Destination.

17. I know how to/where to go to get the talents I need to succeed

There are so many places to get professional development. Schools and online courses can help you a lot if you decide to start something on your own. Actual degrees are the only thing that will count if you are trying to get a new job. Recruiters look for experience and degrees. That's pretty much it.

Learning how to reposition your talents and experience on a resume and how to interview for a new career helps. It can be done. I do it for people all of the time.

18. I have innate talents I can use to lead me to my Life Success Destination

    Innate talents are those that come naturally to you, that are easy for you. Do you focus on your strengths? Knowing your weaknesses is helpful, but I always recommend investing in your strengths. It's a lot easier to move forward with them. That's what I do with my clients, figure out what they need to develop more of and help them to get it.

    I have a friend who is one of the most talented people I know. The really great thing about her is she lets everybody know it! She exudes confidence in her talents. Ask her about something and she will tell you how good she is at that. And she speaks so confidently about it, you automatically believe her!

I think more people should let people know what they are good at and not feel like they are bragging. Just showing confidence!

19. I am maximizing the use of all the talents I have

Do you push yourself to new breakthrough levels using your talents to achieve more, or do you settle for what you can do now?

One common situation is when someone's life and career is out of their control.

Everybody has problems to face that can affect work. Now it's harder than ever.

Jeanine was another one of my really good success stories. She had a big corporate job as a VP of IT. **She had to take a leave, first to take care of her Dad with Alzheimer's Disease. After he died, her Mom developed it as well.**

She spent 7 years taking care of her parents and then was completely out of money and could not find a job doing what she used to do after they passed.

Jeanine used to make over $250,000/year as a VP Information Technology for a large company.

After 7 years away from her work, no one would look at her resume. She was out of the workforce too long. Her field, technology, had changed.

She found us and we worked with her to help her realize she still had a great future, maybe not at the same level, but she has a great future

She does have great IT talents, but they would be hard to sell after 7 years out of it. Things change, and companies are reluctant to hire people who have taken long leaves of absence.

We worked to identify all her talents and to reposition her resume for different opportunities. She has great marketing talents she never recognized from her job as a VP IT.

Quickly I was able to get her into a great job selling IT work for an IT services company. Realizing she didn't need a job managing a whole bunch of people, she quickly went back to work doing something she loved, marketing and selling for a company who really valued her talents. She did have to start at a much lower salary than she used to make, but she had a new start.

Jeanine was so successful off the bat, the company was thrilled with her results because she could call on high level people in companies and talk about how her new company could help them because she really knew it. She used to be in the job of the person she is now selling to!

Win-win for Jeanine and for her new company. She's making a lot of money now for them and they are paying her a good base and much more in bonuses! Title, level, and management responsibility aren't everything. There's a lot of ways to use your same talents to make money.

Jeanine made a great re-start of her career and I felt really good about getting her to a place she was proud to be.

20. I use the talents I have to help others succeed

If you have a strong TAP you can use talents both in your career and to volunteer or to teach others.

Don't underestimate the importance of doing this as part of your overall journey to reach your Life Success Destination.

There are a lot of volunteer opportunities out there. I believe there are two ways that will benefit you and the ones you are volunteering to help.

First, find opportunities that focus on what you do best. Share the talents you have by teaching others what you know, then you are changing their future and strengthening what you have.

Second look for opportunities for volunteer positions that will challenge you to develop your talents or to develop new ones. It's a whole lot easier to convince a volunteer organization to hire you (let you work there for free) than a for-profit company.

Long-term volunteer positions (where you have real responsibilities) will help you some on your resume if you are looking to break into a new career.

ACTION STEPS I WILL TAKE TO INCREASE MY SCORE

ON THE TALENT GAUGE:

Looking at your answers for questions 11 through 20, what can you do to get a full star on this gauge? THESE ANSWERS WILL FORM YOUR MAP TO YOUR LIFE SUCCESS DESTINATION!

11. I know what my best talents are to reach my Life Success Destination

One basic way to start is to think about your talents is to select one of your best accomplishments. What was that?

The last strong work accomplishment I had was:

The talents I used to accomplish that were:

1.

2.

3.

Get a copy of job requirements for the type of work you really want to do. It's easy: Go to any job site and look up your ideal job and it will give you the employer's list of requirements.

Now, what are the gaps? (What are you missing?)

Those are the ones you will need to develop.
It's easier to work in jobs that your initial TAP is scored in the first two columns, High and Medium.

12 I know how to develop my current talents

How will you do it?

13. I know what additional talents I need to achieve my Life Success Destination

    A.

    B.

    C.

    D.

    E.

14. My current talents are all I need to move up to a higher level position

How do you plan to do that?
- Who defines your talents?
- Your company, job description, performance appraisal? Only if you want to stay there. Because that's just the talents they need from you.
- You probably do not think about your real talents. The ones you have that can guarantee your Life Success.

COMPLETE YOUR OWN TAP CHART HERE

Write in your top 5 current talents, rate them, and draw the columns.

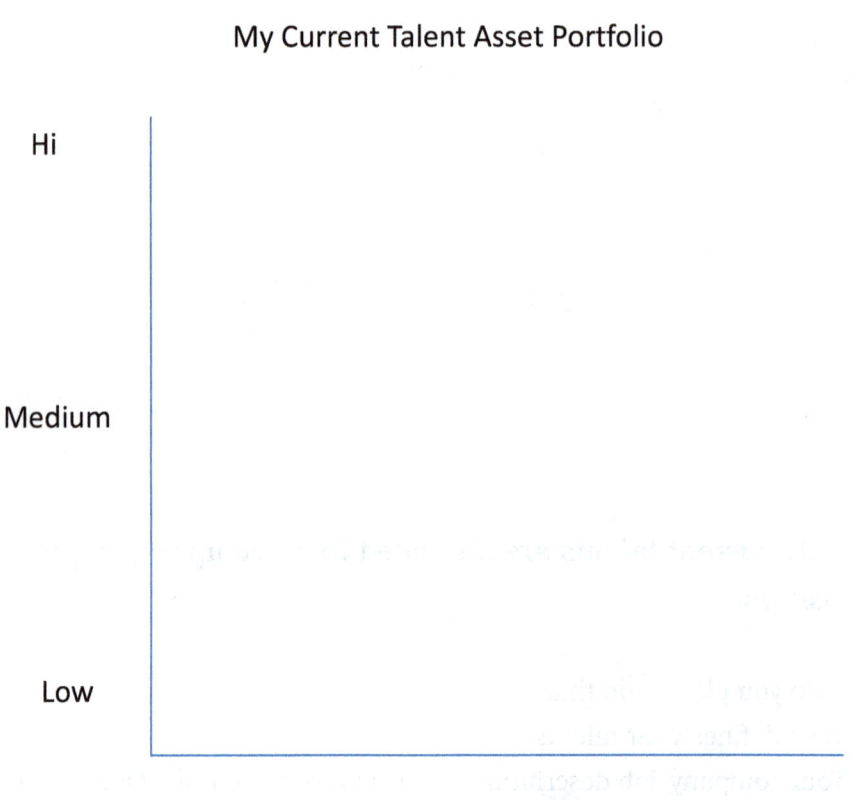

Now write in the names of the talents you will need and draw the columns according to the levels that will be needed. Compare the two charts

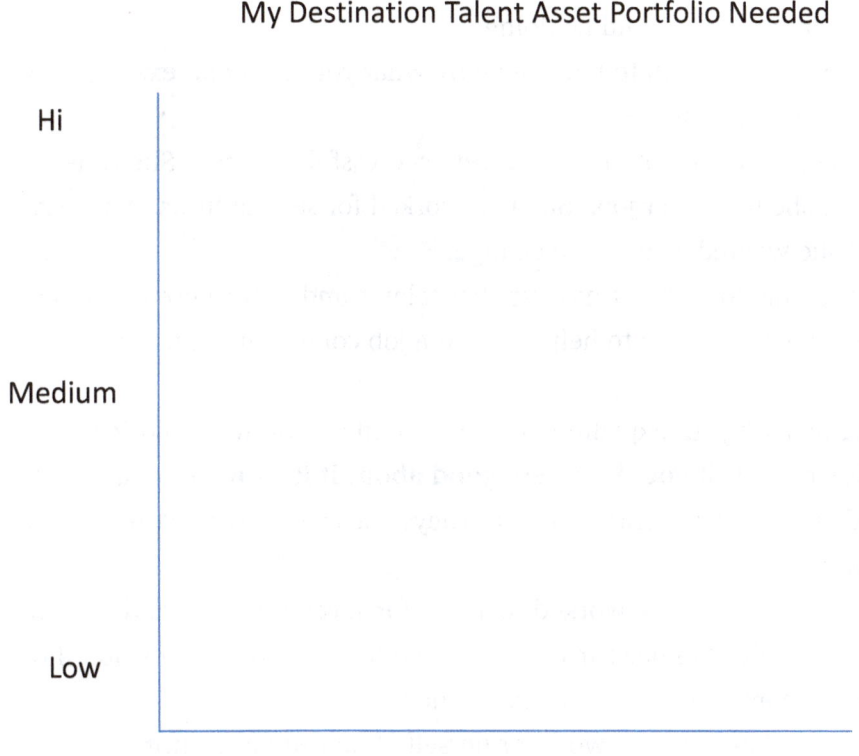

Confidence comes when you know what you are good at, and then put those talents to work

It's simple once you see them.

15. I am confident I can change careers if I want to with the talents I have

I frequently work with people who have realized they are just tired of the "same old same old" job.

Perhaps you are stable and secure but just not feeling like you've found your Life Success? Not unhappy, but not happy either?

It's very common. Just doing the same thing day after day and not knowing what else you could be doing.

I advise having a plan to know **exactly** what you want and **exactly** how you are going to get there.

A good example was Katherine, a very successful attorney. She called me because she hated her job. She had worked for several firms. She was clear that she wanted a complete change.

She hired me to help her discover her talents and how to use them in a new role. She wanted me to help her find a job completely different from law.

Being in a job you're qualified for, very good at, and well paid for is hard to leave. **But if you don't feel good about it it's time to change.** I do hear that pretty frequently from attorneys – it's a very conflict-based job and not a lot of fun!

In Katherine's case, we worked together for several months to distill out all that was involved in her current work, and how we could transition those talents into a completely different career field.

She knew didn't want to work for herself. I helped her identify completely different opportunities she was really qualified to do.

She had many responsibilities and talents in her lawyer job. I suggested she reposition her career in law to a career in communications. It is what she was really good at, was a big part of her job, and the parts she enjoyed the most. She communicated with all levels of people. Clients, companies, other lawyers and she had to know how to represent her client by clearly communicating each case. I needed to find her a job using what she was best at, but in a lower conflict based environment.

I repositioned her resume and prepared her for each of her interviews. I believe each interview requires specific preparation for the best outcome.

Now Katherine works for a large company in charge of their communications department and she loves it! She does not miss law at all!! She was really a fun client to work with because she was so dedicated to making a change and willing to do what it took to do it.

16. My current talents will allow me to keep my job stability if I want to prepare to work for myself

Can you do both?

17. I know how to/where to go to get the talents I need to succeed:

How?

Where?

18. I have innate talents I can use to lead me to my Life Success Destination

What are they?

19. I am maximizing the use of all the talents I have

How I am doing that:

20. I use the talents I have to help others succeed

What? Where? How?

How will doing that will help my career?

The training function can be a really big function. In one company I had 50 Directors of Training reporting to me across 130 brands for 100 different companies all coming together in our corporate office.

In another company I had 150 trainers responsible for training all levels of people who reported to me and I also had 150 recruiters.

In each company I learned what is required to be successful in all levels of jobs. I was responsible for all of them, top to bottom. Hiring people and developing them.

It is such an important responsibility to choose people who will do well and be happy in a particular position.

In my work, I took it very seriously because I saw the consequences of what happened when people failed due to poor fit.

Having been responsible for the careers of hundreds of thousands of people from entry level to CEO, I know each job with a unique person in it is different. But most companies don't see it that way. They slot people into job requirements the best they can with the talents they think they have.

But *each person* has their own responsibility as well.

You have the responsibility to select what will be the best for you! How have *you* done so far?

Cartoon by Jack Gentry

IS THIS HOW YOU PICKED YOUR MAJOR?

Come on, let's be honest. How did you really pick what field you were going into? Write it down.

I won the Chemistry award in my high school the year I graduated. I went to college as a Chemistry major. I got upset with one test grade (the professor messed up and would not change it) and I changed to Business. That was it. One grade changed my major.

Turns out my talents always would be better in Business.

IS THIS HOW YOU PICKED YOUR CAREER?

What about you? Write down exactly how you ended up in the career you are in.

I am not a believer in vocational testing. I think they do more harm than good to people trying to pick a career. They are great at telling you what you should not do and I think that is a big disservice. There are much better ways to pick a career.

Talent Asset Portfolio™

For Life Success

Each person has a unique Talent Asset Portfolio. There are different levels of talents, just like your TAP shows. I start with a person's natural talents, those that are innate. They will be the strongest.

When I work with clients we inevitably discover that they have a whole lot of talents that can't be seen, like the iceberg. You have so much to work with. Start with what you know you have.

The more assets you have in your portfolio, the more you have to manage. They need to be analyzed and you have to decide which ones to develop. **It's important to keep up with what is going up, what is going**

down in value, what to hold, and what to invest more in. Just like a stock portfolio.

Do you know what's in your portfolio? Do you know how to take charge of it, to manage it daily, like they are the most important assets you have?

Do you know which are the most valuable to you and to others?

Your Best Talent?

When I was head of Executive Development for a very large international company I had the pleasure of meeting one of the most impressive women I've ever met.

Responsible for Executive Resources, I also I led a group in the company for executive women (anyone Director and above) and we had monthly events. We invited Frances Hesselbein to speak at one of our events.

Frances is the former CEO of the Girl Scouts and led the organization for 14 years. A huge organization.

Frances started in 1965 as a volunteer troop leader and in 1976 she took over as CEO for another 14 years. During her tenure the Girl Scouts grew to a membership of 2.25 million girls and a volunteer staff of 780,000. That's a lot of people to lead!

In 1990 she left to run the Leader to Leader Institute, started by Peter Drucker, the most famous management professor and writer. After Drucker's death in 2005, it was renamed for her and she continued to run huge leadership functions for large companies.

She founded lots of other organizations. She wrote 27 books published in 29 languages around the world. She also was awarded the Presidential Medal of Freedom in 1998.

Here's the amazing part, Frances never finished college. In fact, she only took a few classes at a junior college in 1936. That was it.

Today, Frances is 105 years old. She still sits on several very prestigious company and social boards and is very active.

The evening before she was to speak we invited attendees to one of our director's homes for a welcome cocktail party.

Frances came up to me, (she had no idea I was in charge of the group) looked at my name tag and said in a very forthright manner: "Deborah Gentry, D for Determined! You are a very determined woman!"

I was so impressed that she took less than a second to come up with that. I have no idea if she said something like that to everyone she meets (maybe she has one for each letter of the alphabet, like sweet for Sarah?" I'll bet at 105 years old she still does that.

Anyway, she was delightful to talk to and I've never forgotten what she said to me.

In fact, she was right. Being determined is my best talent, my best asset and it's gotten me to my Life Success Destinations.

I have spent my entire career helping people to identify their best talents and to develop them. Frances spent her career encouraging people to use their best talent.

What is your best talent? Remember to use it today.

This is a picture of a box I keep on my desk.

What would you do if you thought this? Can you do it now to get moving toward your Destination?

Your Destiny *should be* **your Life Success Destination. But you have to build your Talent Asset Portfolio to get there.**

Answer this question: What my Life Success Destination means to me.

Each person has a unique TAP and a unique Life Success Destination. That's why I work with people one-on-one.

CHAPTER 6

OUTLOOK GAUGE

Outlook

**You can make a living
Or you can make your Life Success
Dr. Deborah—**

It ALL depends on your OUTLOOK. What you want and if you can really see yourself getting there. What do you have in mind? Work that is meaningful to you?

If you see all the negatives you will be trapped in that negative Outlook. If you have the confidence you can get there then you see the promise of the future.

Surround yourself with positive people who want the best for you. What you think about IS your Outlook. Give yourself a rich Outlook.

THE ASSESSMENT QUESTIONS FOR OUTLOOK:

21. I know I can achieve my Life Success Destination if I am dedicated to it

What you think about matters. If you think you can, you can. If you doubt yourself, it will be a lot harder.

It's all about SELF-CONFIDENCE, convincing yourself you can do it.

How do you build confidence? By doing something to move in the right direction everyday. Day by day you are building a track record to be proud of and before you know it, you have confidence.

22. I have high expectations for myself and my future

It certainly is better to have high expectations of yourself if you want to succeed. If you don't expect much, you won't get much.

Are you "Small minded" or "Big-minded"?

Understand that being "Big-minded" might mean you have to give up some things to make big changes. Giving up some time on the things you like to do such as giving up TV. Giving up sports for a while. You will have to change your schedule to accomplish "Big-Minded" things. Getting up earlier, giving up reading the paper or watching the news (it's all bad anyway) to get a fast start everyday. This is what it takes.

You have to determine what high expectations means for you. I guarantee you'll have a lot more fun if you go Big.

23 I am very happy with my job/career/business

Happiness with your work is a key indicator you are on the road to your Life Success Destination. If you have that, you have a lot. And since this is how you spend the majority of your TIME, it is much more enjoyable.

However, it will change with different phases of your life. Sometimes a job is perfect for you, maybe right out of school. Then, later you realize it's not. You can't even believe you spent so many years at it so far. What to do now?

This question definitely affects whether you have a 2 star or a 5 star Life Success Destination.

In my coaching experience, people have a completely different framework of work happiness depending upon whether they move from job to job, are in a career of similar jobs, or have their own business.

Generally having more independence equates with more happiness with work.

This is a good indicator that you are satisfied with the overall situation you are in with your work.

Feeling like you are in a good environment working with people you like and for an organization with products/services/mission you like means a lot. You feel like your TIME is being well-spent working on something worthwhile and with people you like being with. It makes the workday more enjoyable.

24. I believe there is a lot of opportunity ahead of me

It's hard to believe if you don't have a good sense of where you are going.

LIFE SUCCESS IS BEST WHEN YOU ARE IN CHARGE OF IT

Many jobs require repetition of some tasks, over and over again. It's hard to be creative and to think if you don't feel a lot of meaning in your work. Is your work providing something meaningful to others? If not, now may be a good time to see the opportunities you can develop for yourself.

It feels good to think about the future. Psychology studies conclude that thinking nostalgic thoughts lead to focusing on losing what was. Thinking about the future allows you to think about being in control. Having a forward-looking Outlook will allow you to create your opportunities.

25. My career is progressing the way I want it to

As long as your career really is the way *you* want it to be, not what your boss or others want it to be, then you are in a great position to keep moving toward your Life Success.

26. I am willing to take risks, even fail at times, to achieve my ultimate outcomes

Are you comfortable with the unknown? It can be hard. The way to overcome that is to determine your future as much as you can by planning what it will be and making sure you have options.

What you think about expands your potential. You can choose to change your Outlook.

If you focus on what could go wrong, you won't take any chances. You can miss out on your future.

27. I have a sense of adventure

Give yourself a gift an exciting outlook.

Not a small version, but a big version of what you can do. A negative or limiting Outlook will shut down your future.

28. I am living life on my own terms and have the independence I need to be successful

What does that look like? Is it being able to determine what your work is, who you work for, when you do it, and how your work is done? Do you want more vacation time? Less work travel? Being able to make your own decisions?

WEAR YOUR LIFE SUCCESS

Everyday, do you *look like* you are on your way to your Life Success Destination? Do you look and feel the part?

Do you feel good about you, about the way you look, the way you move, the way you dress what you eat and drink? Looking your best is a big part of this. **You should continue to be your best in all areas of your life while you work toward your Destination.** You have to show confidence all along the way. If your goal is to be a millionaire, look like it now (that is not a license to shop). You can look like "a million bucks" just by looking your best everyday.

Wearing your Life Success NOW will improve your image. You will show others what success looks like!

29. I am moving forward on my journey to Life Success

You need to know where you are now so you'll know when you are moving forward. Are you keeping track of your mile markers?

30. I really love my life as it is and I am happy

What a wonderful place to be! A positive and joyful attitude is important.

However, we know there is always room for making anything even better. If you really are happy with where you are now, you will be happy with your journey to Life Success.

"If you're happy and you know it, clap your hands!"

Remember that **LIFE SUCCESS IS DIFFERENT FROM** WHAT PEOPLE NORMALLY THINK OF WHEN THEY ENVISION SUCCESS.

The Success Tightrope

ACTION STEPS I WILL TAKE TO INCREASE MY SCORE

ON THE OUTLOOK GAUGE:

Looking at your answers for questions 21 through 30, what can you do to get a full star on this gauge? THESE ANSWERS WILL FORM YOUR MAP TO YOUR LIFE SUCCESS DESTINATION!

21. I know I can achieve my Life Success Destination if I am dedicated to it

Are you willing to do whatever it takes? How much time? Investment?

22. I have high expectations for myself and my future

What are your goals?

How successful do you want to be?

What do you want to be able to get? Houses, cars, resources for business?

How will you be able to use your success to help others?

23 I am very happy with my job/career/business

If you are, congratulations! If you see room to be even more happy, write down how you plan to do it.

If you are not, what can you do about it?

24. I believe there is a lot of opportunity ahead of me

What are those opportunities? When will you get them?

25. My career is progressing the way I want it to

If not, what do you want in your career progression and when?

26. I am willing to take risks, even fail at times, to achieve my ultimate outcomes

Be specific about what risks you are willing to take.

27. I have a sense of adventure

How does this sense of adventure figure into your Life Success?

28. I am living life on my own terms and have the independence I need to be successful.

If not, why not? How does that affect your Outlook?
How can you change that if you want to?

DO YOU GET TO WORK ON YOUR OWN TERMS?

29. I am moving forward on my journey to Life Success

If you think you are, how do you know you are?

30. I really love my life as it is and I am happy

It's always good to capture what you think about your life and happiness now so you can reflect back on it later. Write how you feel about this now.

Your History is not Your Destiny. Your Destiny can be your Life Success Destination

—Dr. Deborah

YOU CAN CONTROL YOUR LIFE SUCCESS DESTINATION!

The most difficult coaching clients I have are those who just want to wallow in their current circumstances, and often in their past. You must be able to **let go** of where you are and realize you won't be able to leave there if you don't. Planning for your Life Success Destination is fun. Nothing scary about it!

I like to use the word, Destiny, because **your future *is* your Destiny**. How your life turns out *is* your Destiny. You can use what you have been given to influence that. You will see a Christian influence in all of my work, and I want to clarify that God gives you free will. He does not determine your destiny. You do. He gives you what you need to succeed. You are born with talents and you can and should add to them. It is up to you to get to your destination.

STOP CHASING SUCCESS SCHEMES

Some people spend their whole lives chasing success. Looking for the new best deal. Investing in this or that. Trying everything from network marketing to doing deals with people who really haven't even achieved success for themselves.

Investing in yourself is the best way to achieve your own success. It is the best probability of getting to your Life Success Destination. Bet on yourself rather than others. It will be **your plan** and **it will** be achieved.

Anyone who wants to do this must be **Forward Focused**. No time for worrying about the past, **you're not going there**. It's just a distraction keeping you from achieving your dreams.

The dictionary definition of the word "Forward" is: "In the direction that one is facing or traveling." Also defined with the word "Onward" which means to make progress toward a successful conclusion.

Where are you facing or traveling? To your Life Success Destination?

If so, you will need to stop worrying. It takes up too much energy and won't get you where you want to go. **You need to use your energy for creativity, not being annoyed or frustrated. Be grateful you have the chance to control your own future. MOVE FORWARD AND ONWARD! That is your direction to your Destination.**

EXPECT THE BEST FOR YOURSELF

Do you feel like you are going nowhere? Maybe that's why you are reading this book. If you want to change course you must change directions. Change your Outlook.

Coming to the realization of being at a dead-end, fenced-in with no alternatives, is a devastating feeling. And very stressful. Are you willing to make the decision to jump the fence or stay where you are? It takes courage and determination to make that decision.

I saw a car that has a bumper sticker that says:
Boldly Going Nowhere

At first, I laughed.
Then I quickly realized this is a bumper sticker that represents too many people. People who are just blindly going from one day to the next. Working very hard. BOLDLY. Just expecting that tomorrow will bring the same as today and yesterday. Does this sound familiar?

Maybe I should use it as our "Anti-tag line!" People *I* work with would have a bumper sticker that says:

"GOING BOLDLY <u>SOMEWHERE</u>"

This is a very big difference. Because you will end up wherever you *expect* to go.

Do you want to go Nowhere or to your Life Success Destination?

If you don't know exactly where that is yet, at least you've reached a conclusion that you need a change.

Where are you going? Decide if you want a 1, 2, 3, 4, or 5 Star Destination.

Just be "Boldly Going Somewhere!"

All futures come with risk. There is no way to completely eliminate uncertainty. But that is where the fun is. That is where your biggest potential lies. *You can't just "stay in your lane."* **You won't be able to plan every single detail. You might even have to create your own highway. If you insist on a future based on certainty, no disappointments no surprises, you will end up with less than if you step out with passion.**

My program is meant to take calculated risk because you will have filled up all your tanks with the best talents you have. That gives a level of predictability, but not complete certainty. You have to be prepared.

Boldly Going Somewhere requires passion and determination to get there. There is a fear of the unknown, but living a life *without* passion is also something to be afraid of.

BOLDLY GOING SOMEWHERE

EXPECT MIRACLES EVERYDAY.

The fact that you wake up everyday is a miracle. Why not wake up with a positive attitude? Its' a much more enjoyable way to live. If you wake up looking for problems, you will find them!

Who has the better chance of success:

Someone who has negative focus and worries all the time, or someone who has a positive outlook and EXPECTS good things to happen?

EXPECT the best to happen and it will!

CHART A NEW ROUTE

To get to your 5 Star Life Success Destination, you may have to change the route you are on.

You may have to get off the 2 lane road and jump onto an Interstate. That also means not traveling the same old roads over and over again. If you haven't achieved your Life Success Destination on the road you are on, *it's time to get off!!*

The way to do that is to plan for being what I call a "Hi-Po". In every one of my jobs I was responsible for evaluating all of the talent in the organization. I'd do an in-depth assessment of the top 1000 to identify the High Potentials. It took days to conduct each one as part of a program.

Those were the people we would invest in developing. I arranged extra training, more education, and special assignments within the company to prepare them for their next move.

THINK OF YOURSELF AS A HI-PO!!! Develop your own potential to get where you want to be inside or outside of an organization.

OUTLOOK REQUIRES strategic planning. Just like a company has a strategic plan to achieve objectives, so should you.

Fail to plan, plan to fail.

For some people their Life Success Plan is they hope to win the lottery. Hope is not a plan.

I always start a coaching client with two questions: "How did you get here?" then follow up with "How do you plan to move forward in your Life Success?"

Those two questions are very revealing as to OUTLOOK. Most people will tell a story that basically amounts to, "I graduated, took job X then moved to job Y now in job Z. Never thought about it, just took whatever came my way. Don't know what will come my way next."

Unfortunately, that explains why many end up where they are—NOT AT THEIR 5 STAR LIFE SUCCESS DESTINATION.

Trying to figure everything out alone is the fastest way to stay stuck where you are.

LIFE SUCCESS IS NOT A LOTTERY. If you plan to have a great life, you will need to set yourself up to **go in the direction** you want to go!

Determination is definitely an aspect of Outlook. Just like Frances told me I AM "Determined Deborah". Having a Determined Outlook is proven to get you results and also a big advantage to happiness. Medical Science has many studies on how being determined leads to a healthier outcome. Going into a difficult medical situation being depressed or expecting a bad outcome is more likely to end up worse for the patient.

I believe Determination is part of your spirit, and having a positive energized spirit will get you to your Life Success Destination. Having a negative spirit (a lack of determination) will get you nowhere.

How do you use your mind to go where you want to go?

PRIORITIES OF MANAGEMENT (POM)

VS

PRIORITIES OF MINE (POM)

After my corporate career I focused primarily on helping people achieve their success through their careers; how to choose their work. Should they work for companies, organizations, or for themselves? What is an individual's best route to Life Success?

When I started my own consulting/coaching firm, several of the presidents I worked with in prior companies asked me to continue to work with them in new companies they had joined. I realized I could help them with both POM's.

Whenever I worked with individuals I was able to blend coaching what was important to their career *and* their overall Life Success.

What was interesting is how much it takes to get someone out of the realm of doing everything just for an organization. Corporate people become ingrained with thinking that their success is synonymous with the organizations's success. THAT SIMPLY IS NOT TRUE. It's very very hard to get a Five Star Life Success Destination working solely for someone else.

The U.S. Bureau of Labor Statistics says that the median number of years that employees have worked for their current employer is currently 4.1 years, however, this longevity varies by age and occupation. The median tenure for workers ages 25 to 34 is 2.8 years.

But the overall average tenure is about 3 years with anyone company. Exec-U-Net does quarterly surveys and they say that even for executives making over 100k/year the average is now 3 to 5 years that an executive stays with one company.

Pretty amazing! That definitely syncs with my experience in working with people. And because of that most companies no longer invest in developing people for the next job since they don't expect to keep them long enough to pay for the expense!!!

Look around you and see for yourself. How many people have been in their job with one company for more than 3 years? Probably the ones making the least money because those are the ones who get kept to do the same job for long periods of time.

SO how can you plan your Life Success Destination when you can't plan on any one job lasting more than about 3 years?????

You can't depend on job security and advancement alone to get you there

Inhale the future
Exhale the past

CHAPTER 7

MONEY GAUGE

Face it, the world revolves around money. Do you know how to make money? Can you make money on your own if necessary? How to manage money? Do you have control of your income? Do you have a long term plan? Can you comfortably take care of yourself, your family, and others? Do you have access to financial resources? Are you good at managing the money you have?

All the books and survey's I've read about happiness conclude that indeed, Money *can buy* Happiness. Not that the more money you have the happier you will be. But NOT having the money you need causes *unhappiness*. Millionaires overall score higher on happiness.

THE ASSESSMENT QUESTIONS FOR MONEY:

31. I want to make a lot of money

That is a fine goal! Nothing wrong with that!

To get there you more than likely need to invest in yourself. Never feel like that's selfish because it's not. Investing in yourself is investing in your future Life Success. Rarely will someone else do it for you. Do it for yourself so you can make a lot of money!

32. I know why I want to make a lot of money

Some people want to make a lot of money as a scorecard, an accomplishment.
* To prove something to someone
* To prove worth to myself. I have value
* Others just want to be comfortable
* Some want it for security
* Others for freedom
* To change someone's life for the better

33. I believe being wealthy would be good for me

Money gives you options

Money <u>can</u> buy happiness

Poverty certainly does not buy happiness

34. I feel confident in my financial plan for my Life Success

Managing money and planning how to make more is very important. Making it is one thing, holding onto it is another.

Saving money is hard. The world has thousands of ways to get you to spend your money. Think about every hundred dollars you could put to use for your future Life Success and put it there, not into spending.

Most financial counselors will tell you to invest it. I know how important it is to have a substantial amount of money put in a place for emergencies or to grow your business.

35. I already have the financial resources I need for the way I want to live in the future

Yes or no determines what you need to do.
If no, you'll need to start making more, saving more.

36. I understand how important money is to get to my Life Success Destination for myself, my family, and for others

This section started with "the world revolves around money." It's true for every aspect of our daily lives. It is important and understanding *how* important it is for *your* Life Success will help you to move forward.

37. I know how to make money on my own

I designed classes on this when I worked for a very large company and the CEO wanted every single person in management to understand the process of how to make money. But of course it was making money for the company.

To make money on your own you have three ways:

1. *Sell your time*

2. *Sell a service*

3. *Sell a product*

I have worked with many people explaining these three things. It really is a whole separate book. For this purpose just know that if you are selling your time as an employee you are limited. If you are selling your time as a consultant, as a 1099, you have a lot more control over your future.

Selling a service or a product can be lots of fun if you have the talents for sales. Also a whole other book!

38. I am comfortable making lots of money because I know its good for me and to help others

Believe it or not there are a lot of people *not* comfortable making lots of money. I've met them. For some reason they have grown up thinking that money is bad, does bad things to people. I have no idea where that comes from. It prevents them from striving for any kind of success that has money attached to it. This is definitely *not* the way to Life Success.

39. I am on target to make enough money to take care of myself, my family, and others

If you can answer yes to this, then you will have more freedom to get to Life Success Destination. If not, you'll be inspired even more to start the journey so you can have enough for those you care about.

40. I do not want to worry about money and where it will come from

You won't have to work for the money just to have the money. It's not about greed.

Money brings FINANCIAL FREEDOM. Not having money brings worry and instability. *Money by itself is not the goal.* But having money brings financial freedom to do what you want **which is the goal** most people dream of.

You also need to learn how to secure your money/invest it in your future, to be able to keep your financial freedom.

WOULDN'T THAT BE A PEACEFUL WAY TO

WAKE UP EVERYDAY?

ACTION STEPS I WILL TAKE TO INCREASE MY SCORE

ON THE MONEY GAUGE:

Looking at your answers for questions 31 through 40, what can you do to get a full star on this gauge?

THESE ANSWERS WILL FORM YOUR MAP TO YOUR LIFE SUCCESS DESTINATION!

31. I want to make a lot of money

Journal that right here so you can reflect back on your answer as you work toward getting to your Life Success Destination: Yes or No?

32. I know why I want to make a lot of money

Give your answer more detail here so later on when you have all your Life Success you can look back and remember your reasons:

33. I believe being wealthy would be good for me

This is a fun one to visualize if you are not already wealthy. Imagine yourself having a million dollars. What will you do with it?

1.

2.

3.

FILL UP THOSE TANKS — GET ALL GAUGES UP TO GET YOUR 5 STARS!

Imagine having a *hundred* million dollars. How will you use it?

1.

2.

3.

4.

5.

34. I feel confident in my financial plan for my Life Success

What is your plan? Does it include investing in yourself? In your talents? It should. Investing in yourself is never selfish. Even if your family had something else they wanted to do with the money you may have to spend on a course or a program. Put it in your plan.

35. I already have the financial resources I need for the way I want to live in the future

Do you?

36. I understand how important money is to get to my Life Success Destination for myself, my family, and for others

Why is it important for your specific plan to get there?

37. I know how to make money on my own

If you are interested in your Life Success, I'll bet you already have ideas on how to make money.

What are they?
1.

2.

3.

4.

5.

38. I am comfortable making lots of money because I know its good for me and to help others.
Comment on why it will be good/who it's good for.

39. I am on target to make enough money to take care of myself, my family, and others.
Are you? If not, how far away are you?

40. I do not want to worry about money and where it will come from.

Well who wants to worry about money? Not you!

When I was working for corporations and getting my three weeks of vacation a year (NEVER ENOUGH VACATION!) we would take one week and go to a very fancy condo complex on the beach in Florida. Most of the people owned their own condo and all knew each other.

Each day by the pool I could hear a group of retired guys talking about what they were going to do that day.

Each talking about going to golf, swim in the pool, swim in the ocean, dinner out to a different restaurant each night. They never once referred to their past. Never talked about old times at work.

I asked someone about what their careers were and no one knew.

Being head of HR I was always interested in what someone did now or in the past. What was their job? Who did they work for? How long? Where?

But it didn't matter.

What mattered was that they had enough money and good health to enjoy life and move forward. They could do whatever they wanted. They could start businesses or just golf.

Here's the point:

MONEY IS A BIG FACTOR. IT'S THE BIGGEST FACTOR IN DETERMINING HOW YOU WILL LIVE YOUR FUTURE LIFE SUCCESS. YOUR MONEY GAUGE NEEDS TO BE FILLED UP.

MONEY OVERRIDES JOB TITLE ANYDAY

When your jobs/career ends (maybe it won't) you won't have a place to go to work unless you have created your own work. No one will care about how big your office was or how many people worked for you. No one will care what your job title was. All of a sudden you will realize — it just doesn't matter. This is a good thing to think about for your future. What is important today won't be the same as what's important for your future. Plan for that now.

IF you have reached your Destination with a good solid financial base you'll have exactly what you need to determine what you want to do.

Go golfing. Go sailing . Go write. Go to your own office. Continue to make money on your own.

CHAPTER 8
RELATIONSHIP GAUGE

Look at this picture. Have you ever seen that going on, or worse, been the recipient?

I certainly have. As head of HR for several multi-billion $ companies I was frequently the target of people's unhappiness.

People are rarely happy with H.R. because H.R. is regularly the bearer of bad news. "No, you are not getting a raise. Your benefits are going to cost more/or are cut back. We're not going to pay for that course. Your performance is not what we want it to be. Your job is being eliminated." On and on.

People's experiences with each other determine whether or not they perceive it as a good or bad relationship. Same at work or home.

THE ASSESSMENT QUESTIONS FOR RELATIONSHIPS:

No one finds Life Success alone

—*Dr. Deborah*

This Gauge is an overall look at where you are with the people who are around you. If you are not totally happy, what can you do?
 a. You can *change your relationships* with the people you are with now.
 b. You can change out the people for new ones. Or at least add new relationships to your existing ones.

41. I have a strong relationship with my boss/es and know they support me and my future plans at work

If you truly have this, you are the lucky and rare employee! It's a great position to be in but you are dependent on them to stay in place and to take care of you. You have to trust they will put your talents to use in more progressive roles as time goes on, even if it is not in their area.
 If not, look elsewhere because it's not going to change.

42. I have people who love and encourage me to pursue my dreams

Do you? It makes this so much easier.

43. My spouse/ family support my work and future goals

Having support at home for your work/career/business is great. Also look for support outside in your community of friends, neighbors, network. You will go a lot farther if you have it.

44. I am totally happy with my family/friend relationships

They are a major influence on your life so being happy with them should mean they support you in any way they can.

45: I invest a lot in my relationships

It's always a two-way street with relationships.

46. I am happy with my peer working relationships

This is definitely an important area to be careful about. I can't tell you how many times I thought I could trust my peers only to find out I couldn't because of competition or jealousy of relationships. This is two parts: your relationship with them, and how they see your relationships with others.

47. I have connections I can count on to help me with a new opportunity

I always encourage people to make connections they can count on and we develop a strategy for them to make the right connections. Who those connections are depends on your plan on how to get to your Destination.

48. I have mentors and coaches I can count on to support my success

If you are employed you may have options at work. Really good mentors are hard to find. Your boss will be wary of anyone else you choose to help you. He/she might or might not be a good choice, for lots of reasons.

    a. They have their own self interest first which means they want you to do well for them and only in your current job
    b. They may not be good at coaching or mentoring
    c. They have favorites and you may or may not be at the top of their list
    d. They will question your motives for asking for their help

You certainly can look inside for people you respect to help you, or outside for an unbiased and expert coach. Make sure to find someone who really knows where you want to go and won't just lead you where *they* want you to go.

49. I have strong network connections in my local and online community

Look into networking groups. They might be a Leads Group or a general business networking group. Also consider joining local organizations. Ask if your company has a representative at the Chamber of Commerce and if you can attend those meetings to network.

50. I can pick up the phone and call someone I don't know to ask for help with my plans

This question is meant to assess your comfort level in reaching out to ask for help. If you aren't comfortable doing that, stick with the people you do know and ask them to make connections for you.

HOW BIG CAN YOUR LIFE SUCCESS BE?

HOW FAR CAN YOU GO?

IT'S UNLIMITED IF YOU JUST START!

You will need support. You will.

Here's a critical component. Get support from your spouse, significant other, and family. **SET YOUR LIFE SUCCESS GOALS TOGETHER.**

SET BIG GOALS TOGETHER. They don't have to be *in* the plan, but they *need to support the plan*. What does that mean?

It may mean sacrificing some things. Like less TV time together, less time with the family. Because you will need to get time from somewhere to accomplish new things to get you where you want to go. Don't go for less sleep or you won't be able to be at your best.

You can have your goals. Your partner/family has her/his goals. But in the middle are the goals you have together which means you two have to agree on that middle part. You don't have to accomplish them together, but you must get support to make that happen. It's fine if your partner/family can't help you with the work. All you need is the decision to GO FOR IT and to agree not to complain about the decisions made.

What is true love? It means supporting the other person in attaining their dreams, and them supporting you in yours. That's what your partner/family should want for you.

This is the secret sauce to the long-term success of your plan. You are not just telling the other person what you need, but you are agreeing on the Life Success Destination and how you are going to get there. Set a target and give updates about how it's going all along the way.

Work: Bosses, co-workers, subordinates, friends

You will need to decide who gets to be a part of getting to your Life Success Destination, and who should not. Be VERY careful of partnering with people at work.

Friends, maybe even some family, won't be supportive and you will have to decide to give up or to move forward without their support. You may have to give up relationships that are holding you back.

Often people will be jealous of your desires to be successful and they will try to hold you back. They will say "You can't do that", but that's only because *they* can't do it. Don't let that happen. Choose who gets to go forward with you and who doesn't.

LIFE SUCCESS

REQUIRES LIFE SUPPORT

ACTION STEPS I WILL TAKE TO INCREASE MY SCORE

ON THE RELATIONSHIP GAUGE:

Looking at your answers for questions 41 through 50, what can you do to get a full star on this gauge? THESE ANSWERS WILL FORM YOUR MAP TO YOUR LIFE SUCCESS DESTINATION!

41. I have a strong relationship with my boss/es and know they support me and my future plans at work

If you are employed, or volunteer, list those people here so you know who will be part of your plan:

    a.

    b.

    c.

    d.

42. I have people who love and encourage me to pursue my dreams

Who are they? What do you need to tell them about your plans?

43. My spouse/family support my work and future goals

How do they support you? Will they support you spending money on your goals? If they don't, what can you do?

44. I am totally happy with my family/friend relationships

Big win if you have a yes on this one. Be sure to include them in on what you are doing. Let them know you are grateful. If you are not happy, what can you do?

45: I invest a lot in my relationships
There are many ways to do this. Giving them your time. Help them with what they are doing.
Who can you help with finding their Life Success Destination?

46. I am happy with my peer working relationships

What are your peer challenges are and how can you address them so you can move forward? Write those here.

47. I have connections I can count on to help me with a new opportunity

Make a list of those connections and plan to contact them. Also note specifically <u>what</u> you want to talk with them about.

WHO AND WHAT:

a.

b.

c.

d.

e.

48. I have mentors and coaches I can count on to support my success

List who they are and answer: Do they know you count on them for guidance? Is it a formal or informal relationship?

How often do you talk about you and your future?

Do you have a plan they can help you with?

a.

b.

c.

d.

49. I have strong network connections in my local and online community

List your network connections:

a.

b.

c.

d.

50. I can pick up the phone and call someone I don't know to ask for help with my plans

If you can, do it. If not, why not? Who can you get to help you contact them?

5 Star Destination

1 Star Destination

Which one do you want?

LIFE SUCCESS DESTINATION

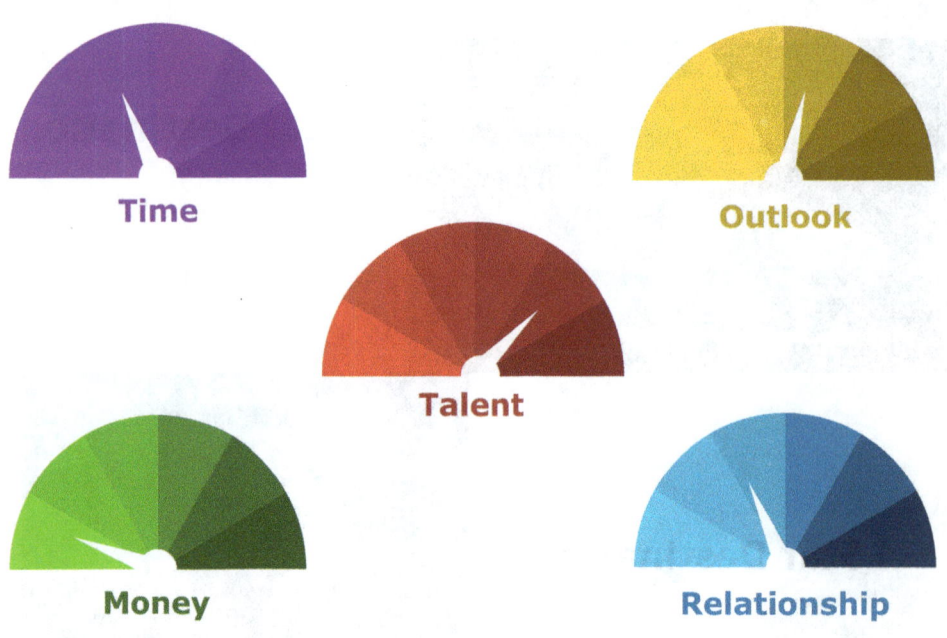

5 GAUGES

LIFE, LIBERTY, AND THE

PURSUIT OF A HIGH LIFE SUCCESS SCORE

In school, did you learn anything about what it means to have a successful life? Did you get any training on what it would take? Did you have any mentors who tried to help you get there? Have you met people you think have achieved Life Success? How do you think they figured it out?

We are all born with the right to pursue Life, Liberty, and Happiness. (At least in the Western World.) You have the right. But do you have the knowledge on how to get there?

I have been working with people to find their own Life Success Destinations for many years. We know from experience that there is not just one route to get there.

YOU MAY HAVE TO CHANGE JOBS TO GET YOUR GAUGES TO 80% OR MORE! YOU MAY WANT TO BECOME INDEPENDENT TO GET YOUR GAUGES OVER 80% TO GET THE LIFE SUCCESS SCORE YOU WANT!

You make decisions everyday. Every decision is a choice as to where you go. You are where you are now as a result of your decisions to this point.

Your Life Success is bigger than where you are now. Once you know your Destination, you will be driven to get there.

WHERE IS YOUR

LIFE SUCCESS DESTINATION?

PART THREE

HOW TO GET TO YOUR

LIFE SUCCESS DESTINATION

CHAPTER 9

DETERMINE WHY AND WHERE YOU WANT TO GO

★★★★★

QUESTIONS TO LEAD YOU

TO THE ANSWER:

What has staying in your current situation cost you in terms of what you are not doing versus what you should be doing?

What are the good things you are missing out on by not being able to live your Life Success?

Are you wasting time from getting where you would rather be? If so, how much time?

Do you dread your current situation? Your current job? Why?

Do you worry about your future?

How will you support yourself? Your family?

What is it costing you mentally, financially and physically to postpone your dream?

How much more do you think you would be earning if you were already at your 5 Star Destination?

$$$$$

Why am I pursuing my Life Success Destination?

Where?
SET YOUR DESTINATION

The Top 3 Destinations

INDEPENDENCE

What would it feel like for you to create a new opportunity for yourself, for you to select and create your Destination? Independent work allows you the control to do that. It gives you control over your lifestyle.

CAREER RENOVATION

Many people think they have landed in the wrong career. Maybe you took a job right out of school, but it wasn't what you wanted to do long-term. Do you feel stifled? How would you like to completely change your career? It takes a clear understanding of what you have to offer now and how to change that into a different career. I know it's possible because I've worked with hundreds of people to do just that.

CAREER PROGRESSION

If you love what you do, but want higher level of responsibilities you can renovate your talents and skills to achieve more in your current organization or to change fields or industries. It does take a lot of preparation. Know it can be done if you want it enough.

SO WHAT ARE YOU GOING TO DO ABOUT IT?

YOU HAVE TO BELIEVE IT CAN HAPPEN BEFORE YOU START.
Believe it is possible and imagine the life you want to have.
Plan <u>Where</u> you want to be, <u>What</u> you want to be doing, <u>When</u> you want to start and <u>How</u> you're going to get there.

Even if you're on the right track,

You'll get run over if you just sit there.

—Will Rogers

WHERE ARE YOU IN YOUR CAREER?

I made this chart to demonstrate how people end up in different jobs in their careers. There are two dimensions. The Positive/Negative dimension and the Voluntary/Involuntary dimension. Perhaps at different times in your life you have been in several of these squares?

VOLUNTARY/NEGATIVE: The square to the top left is the person who voluntarily stays in his/her position. Nothing to look forward to.

Not expecting any upward mobility. Gets minimum raises every year. Some security, could stay doing that job for 40 years. Unfortunately that describes a whole lot of people who get a job and just stay there. They Settle. They Compromise. They are Complacent. Not happy, but OK. Just don't rock the boat.

INVOLUNTARY/NEGATIVE: The square in the bottom left is the person who is in a bad spot because they were caught off guard. In a job that went away, or they got fired. Because they didn't have another plan, they're likely to have a harder time moving to a good option. It's the worst place to be backed into a corner with no where to go, caught by surprise.

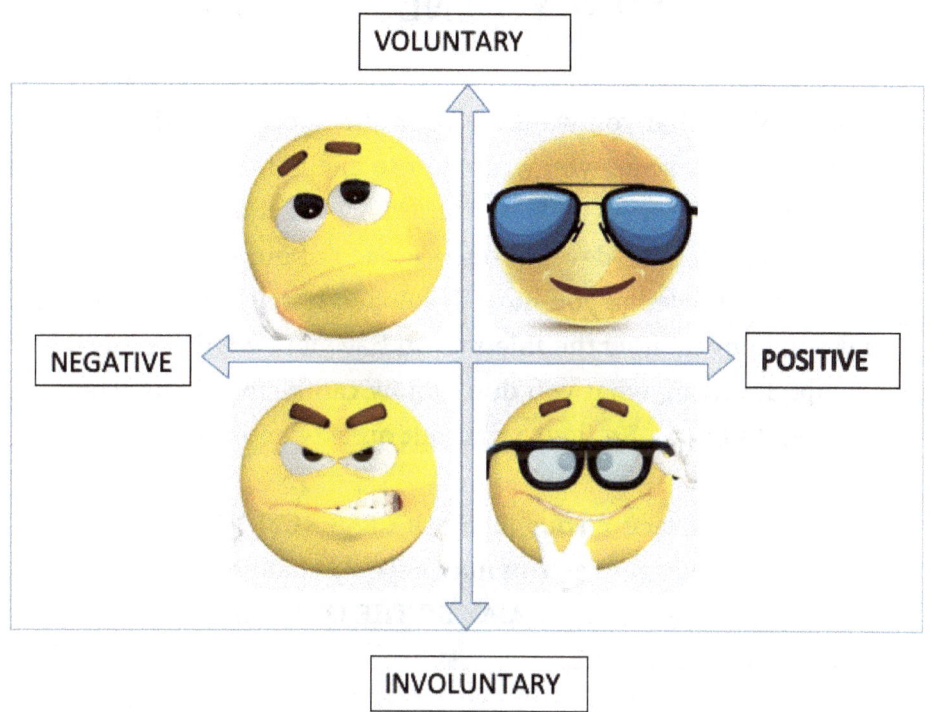

INVOLUNTARY/POSITIVE: This person had an unplanned move, but quickly turned it into a positive. She/He may have been pushed out, but landed well and is happy they got to go somewhere else.

VOLUNTARY/POSITIVE: This person has it made in the shade! He/She was prepared to make a move to their Life Success Destination, or at least headed that direction. They got a great move to a different organization or went out on their own. They decided. They didn't let anyone else decide for them.

Overall you can see how these factors can control your future.

Is it time for you to change *WHILE YOU CAN CALL THE SHOTS*?
Is it time for you to move to the work you were meant to do?
Is it time for you to move toward your Life Success Destination?

Most work surveys I see show about 70% of Americans hate their job. But they don't do anything about it.

WHAT YOU NEED TO DO

1. Determine what you want for your Life Success Destination.
2. Use all the answers you wrote out to each of the 50 questions to develop your LIFE SUCCESS ACTION PLAN which is your MAP to follow everyday. (We develop one for each of our coaching clients).
3. Use the knowledge you have developed here. You need to know what you know. Know the talents you have and what you need to develop. Knowing what you don't know can be more important than what you do know. So figure that out quickly and acquire what you need.
4. Execution: Execute your LIFE SUCCESS ACTION PLAN.

To maximize your gauges you may need to change your environment/job over time. IT MAY BE THE ONLY WAY TO INCREASE YOUR LIFE SUCCESS SCORE.

A bird sitting on a tree is never afraid of the branch breaking because his trust is not on the branch but on his own wings.

Trust your own talents and you will have a more predictable future.

"I'd rather regret the things I've done than regret the things I haven't done."

—*Lucille Ball*

"It's a helluva start, being able to recognize what makes you happy."

— *Lucille Ball*

ENTREPRENEUR?

INDEPENDENT?

I'm amazed at how many people think they are experts telling other people how to be an entrepreneur, when the only business they have ever run is a blog or an Instagram account.

The one thing they all have in common is they tell people to "Find your passion…once you know that, you'll never work again. That's all you need!"

I'm here to tell you as a consultant for many entrepreneurs, and having been one myself plenty of times, **PASSION IS HIGHLY OVERLY RATED,** and has little to do with being a successful entrepreneur. **THERE ARE A LOT OF BROKE, PASSIONATE PEOPLE IN THIS WORLD WHO STARTED BUSINESSES BASED ON THEIR PASSION.**

What does matter in becoming a successful independent or entrepreneur is knowing what you are good at and what you aren't. **Know what's in your TAP.**

These so-called experts/bloggers will say, pursue your passion and find other people to delegate the things you don't know how to do. Or, no worries, just hire a virtual assistant from overseas you will never meet!

Doesn't work that way. Because there are too many things you have to be good at to be successful on your own. You might not be able to afford employees. You might not want to manage them and everything that goes along with having employees.

A good example is a photographer I coached in Texas. He had a passion for photography. Loved landscape photography.

He decided to open a portrait photography studio and put over a $100,000 into a studio. If you've ever had a retail store you know that as a tenant your hours are dictated by the lease, usually you have to be open a minimum of 9 to 6, 7 days a week.

That means you have to have employees to cover the hours. That means you have to be good managing employees. Employees who add a ton to your costs.

Jerry, the photographer, was a great photographer. He hated managing people. To make money to cover all the costs he started providing studio photography for seniors, for children, even did pet photography. The customers were rarely happy because they expected to look better than they did in real life. Jerry spent a ton of time on re-touch trying to make people happy. That was a talent he did not anticipate needing in his business.

Selling is probably the most critical talent that is needed to be an entrepreneur. You have to be able to sell yourself, your work, or your services. Jerry hated selling. He'd rather give away his work than have to ask for money for it. So again, he had to hire someone to sell for him. More expense that could not be covered.

Then came the wedding packages. That seemed like a better way to make more money. Wedding photographers will tell you it's the worst gig of all. Trying to capture something that is only going to happen one time, with the Bridezillas, Bride's mother, and all the other people who really would rather not be there. Not to mention trying to photograph all the drunks at the receptions.

Then there was event photography. Ditto, more drunks.

Jerry didn't have great customer service skills. He was likely to tell customers what he thought! His passion for photography turned into a nightmare business. The only people who got paid were his store employees. Jerry didn't make any money after they were paid.

A good TAP analysis would have shown his strong skills were all on the creative side. Not the administrative or customer service side.

Don't risk not having the right talents.

Poor Jerry, Passionate and Broke!

*GET YOUR **MAP** DIRECTIONS TO YOUR*

LIFE SUCCESS DESTINATION

HOW TO FIND HELP

Look for local groups to help you.

When we were living in Memphis many of the large companies laid off tens of thousands of professionals all at the same time. Memphis is the logistics center of the country and most of those people had only worked in logistics. They had a tough choice, either change industries or change cities.

A group of the people who were laid off started a career-based organization to help the unemployed people affected. They formed 17 different groups with different specialties. Each met once a week. Almost all of them were hosted by churches, anyone could come to any church. The meetings were coordinated through Facebook groups.

Some were early breakfasts with people bringing donuts. A few met at night in restaurants with large meeting rooms. Human Resources consultants in the area volunteered time to go to each meeting, to provide professional advice and support. Each meeting had a sharing time for people to talk about whatever leads they had developed to help each other. It worked quite well. I spoke to very large groups at large churches, and at very small groups in restaurants. It was a great time to learn about what motivates people and how to teach them to make changes.

I was a part of that for several years. I taught resume writing and how to reposition experience for different careers. I also taught how to assess your talents, how to interview, and lots of confidence building classes.

I ended up hiring one of the members to work with my consulting company and then later placed her in a terrific Chamber of Commerce job. People in the groups really bonded with each other and stayed friends for years. I'm still in contact with some of them.

Check around your local city. You may find a group to join like this if you need one.

Later I came up with an idea to host a city-wide event for people looking for new opportunities. It was a very large event in Memphis to put on something that had never been done before. I called it "The Opportunity Expo". I rented an entire museum (the largest one) and all their auditoriums and classrooms. All the newspapers covered it and thousands of people attended. It was free for attendees to come and meet with lots of sponsors I put together to be available to talk about the opportunities they had for people. It was *Not* a job fair. It showcased opportunities sponsors had available as career alternatives. I also had many speakers talk about how people can develop their own opportunities. Leaders of various industries spoke about the future of their companies and where their growth was happening. I spoke as well.

My talk was: PLAN A, B, OR C – WHICH IS BEST FOR YOU? People responded so positively to it, and it seemed to help many who were job hunting. PLAN A, B, OR C continues to be a popular topic helping people.

Looking back I can't believe we pulled it all off with just my husband (Co-Founder of Life Success Channel.com), my daughter who was working on our team, and one of our employees. We had to bring all our own tables, chairs, banners, and signs. I still have many boxes of black tablecloths we bought for the event tables!

I also started a business called Bioworks Place. This was not one of my best businesses. We used the number one recruiting search engine company in our business and I asked them to develop a website/business just like theirs, but unique to Memphis and that would cover all jobs/all industries. My mistake on this one was I assumed we would get local companies to sponsor/pay for listing jobs on our site. I was wrong. Could not give job listings away. It was free for all job seekers. I hired employees, rented office space just for it, spent $300,000 trying to make it work and it failed. Paid for that for a long time.

After that I started a foundation, The Talent Trust Foundation. I recruited a very prestigious board of directors. Our mission was to build a network of very talented people to showcase their skills and let the community know how to find people with those skills. That also didn't work well just because it still was not the right time to find sponsors.

I share the good and the not so good ventures we've had in order to demonstrate that sometimes risk pays off and sometimes it doesn't. But we always kept going until we got it right. You can't succeed if you don't try.

I love helping people move forward in their careers and their lives!

Maybe you have thought of having a business helping other people?

(Photo Credit Instagram)

WALTER MITTY

A really fun movie to use as a Life Success example is "The Secret Life of Walter Mitty". It came out in 2013 but remains a super popular movie because of all the life lessons in it. Even after I give you a quick synopsis, it won't spoil you seeing it.

Walter Mitty is played by Ben Stiller, his mother is Shirley Maclaine and the other main character is the photographer played by Sean Penn (and his character is also named Sean).

Walter's father died when he was 17 and since then (20+ years) his mother and his sister have not worked, depending on Walter for all their income, (MONEY). He's just a photo editor (really a photo processor) working for LIFE Magazine. His RELATIONSHIPS with them are strained and he doesn't seem to have any friends. People at work make fun of him.

LIFE announces they are having a major downsizing and there will only be one more issue. Everyone is worried about being sacked. Walter only knows how to do his job which isn't going to be around anywhere else because everything is going digital.

His job was to handle the works of a super famous photographer (played by Sean Penn) who wanders the world looking for exotic subjects. Walter is worried he will lose his job when he finds out the boss wants to put Sean's final picture on the cover of LIFE magazine, but Walter can't find it. Sean sent it to him but he doesn't know where it is so he sets off to find Sean wherever he is to get the film negative so he can have it for the final cover.

The main theme of the movie is: What is keeping Walter from achieving his dreams? That's what he does all day long is daydream about a life he would like to have, one of adventure and love. But he can't do it.

He can't even get up the courage to ask out a girl he likes from work. He knows what he wants but lacks the confidence and determination it takes to get there, (OUTLOOK + TALENTS).

Little by little throughout the movie Walter must step into different levels of courage as he has to jump out of a helicopter, gets attacked by a shark in Greenland, skate boards down a winding road in Iceland going towards an erupting volcano, and climb mountains in the Himalayas all to track down Sean and get the negative.

Walter is on a tight TIME schedule to meet the magazine's deadline and frantically runs halfway around the world and back looking for the negative. And he has to spend all his own money to do it.

At the end, he finds out he had the negative all along. The movie is really about Walter finding his TALENTS. TALENTS HE DID NOT EVEN KNOW THAT HE HAD to achieve his goal.

The end of the story is really heart-warming and it turns out that Sean's photo was a picture of Walter working (to represent all of the employees at LIFE). That is the photo he was searching for and he didn't know it was a picture of him. It ends up being the cover of the last issue. And of course, now being a new man who discovered his confidence, courage, drive, risk-taking, and determination, Walter walks off with the girl.

The lesson the movie makers were telling was "Stop dreaming about it and go out and do it". They work in the LIFE Magazine motto which is: "To see things thousands of miles away, things hidden behind walls and within rooms, things dangerous to come to, to draw closer, to see and be amazed."

I like to take the end of the movie and come up with the sequel.

Because it's really uncertain. Walter didn't have any experience or talents that will get him a new job. He had three choices:

PLAN A. Look for his job in another company (but all those jobs went away with digital).

PLAN B. Look for a similar job in another industry. What could that be? He could develop the talents he had and look for something different, but sadly, Walter had no clue about what he had to develop.

PLAN C. Walter could go out on his own and be independent. But what would that be??? He didn't know anything he could do on his own, and he's now broke.

Now let's consider the life of Sean, the wildly successful photographer.

Sean knew what his talents were. Walter did not. Even at the end as they walk off, he has nowhere to go and no money left because he spent all he had on the trips to find Sean.

Finding the negative was symbolic of the fact that he already had what he was looking for, but he just didn't know it.

What is Walter going to do now?

At the very end Walter has been fired. He has two dependents and a girlfriend with a little son and she has also been fired. He's unemployed and goes to a coffee shop to work on his resume. He lists all his adventures, but we know none of that will get him a job.

If he gets a similar low-level job he won't make ends meet and will never get to travel again. He'll be chained to another job he doesn't want, dreaming about things he can't afford to do. His time won't be his own.

Walter really felt somewhat important because he was linked to Sean. But now that's over and Sean will keep being famous and making lots of money and Walter won't. Walter is replaceable in that duo. Sean is not. Why?

Because Sean *knows* what his talents are which is why he makes a lot of money and has total freedom to do what he wants, and go where he wants to go. He is the one really living the Life Success dream and he has total power over what he does.

Sean has created something. That's why he's not replaceable.

(Remember Jerry the photographer? He should have followed Sean's Life Success model.)

The photo below is a comment on the moment when after traveling around the world, spending all his money, and taking really big risks, when Walter finds Sean. He asks Sean why he doesn't click the picture and Sean says "I live in the moment" which is a comment on why, after Sean has traveled to the top of nowhere to be able to shoot a photo of the rare ghost cat, he decides not to take the shot, but to live in the moment and see it for real.

If Walter finds another job living paycheck to paycheck like he was before he can't get to his Life Success Destination! His whole past working for LIFE doesn't matter anymore. It's over. His only identity was with them

(Photo credit Instagram)

and it was temporary and was taken away without notice. When LIFE closed, Walter lost everything.

Do you want to be Walter Mitty or Sean?
Sean can sell his pictures to lots of other magazines. He can sell to National Geographic and others. He can print his work and sell it online. He could set up his own stores and sell his collection. He can sell photography books or sell online photography courses. He can continue to have an incredible life and lifestyle that he controls. Because he's built up a

reputation, built up his talents. People know who he is. No one knows who Walter is.

In my opinion, it's better to do Plan C. It's the way to control what happens to your future. Sean had a Plan C.

PLAN C:

One easy way to develop a PLAN C is to develop one of your creative talents. Something you can make money with. A product, service, something people see value in.

Maybe you're a corporate employee but have the desire to be an entrepreneur? Or you're tired of being confined to an office (or a cubicle) knowing you are capable of so much more.

 waltermittymovie

(Photo credit Instagram)

I work with people on designing their PLAN C's and it's really fun to figure it out. There really is a lot to it.

It doesn't take a lot of money to start a business if you know what you're doing. You can make a lot more money *and* have your freedom.

Writing, Coaching, Teaching, Consulting, Training, Graphics are some ideas.

You just have to have your idea. Being successful takes work and you must be willing to put in the effort to get there. You can do it!

WALTER MITTY LESSON: STOP JUST DREAMING ABOUT IT, GO OUT AND DO IT!

GET YOUR TICKET TODAY!

ALL JOBS ARE TEMPORARY AND REPLACEABLE.
DON'T BE REPLACEABLE IF YOU WANT TO BE INDEPENDENT.

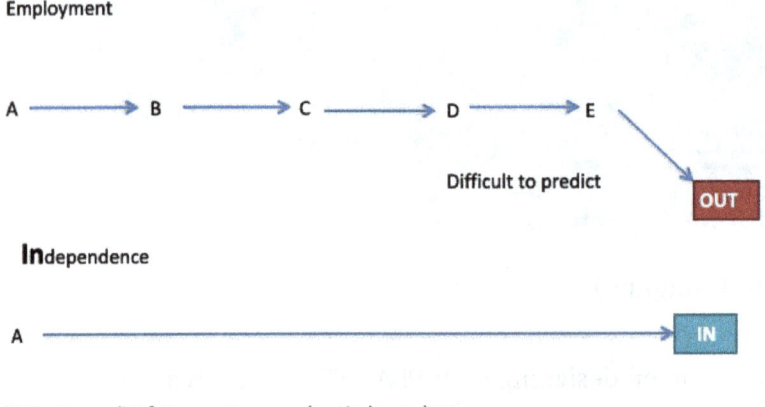

What should you do?

THE ONLY WAY TO TAKE CONTROL OF YOUR FUTURE IS TO BE IN CONTROL OF IT YOURSELF, PERIOD.

If you let others be in control of you, they will ALWAYS do what is best for them, for the company, NOT what is best for you.

If you don't build your own dreams

you will have to continue to work

to build someone else's.

My clients don't have a problem with this! They know where they are going. You can do this!

Denis Waitley is a famous motivational speaker. He was an astronaut and he was a friend of mine. I love this quote of his. He's currently 88 years old, and he has lived a life filled with helping people to succeed through his writing and speaking. At dinner one night just with me and Jack, I'll never forget he said he never gets upset about anything. "Unless someone is threatening me or my family, it's not worth worrying about." I believe that is the key to his long life of Life Success. His career was an independent motivational speaker.

The reason most people never reach their goals is that they don't define them, or ever seriously consider them as believable or achievable. Winners can tell you where they are going, what they plan to do along the way, and who will be sharing the adventure with them.
—Denis Waitley

CHAPTER 10

THE ROAD AHEAD

You will have to think differently than you have in the past. Because the future is different now.
I believe you have a responsibility to deliberately use your talents to become successful, to find your influence and financial freedom.

MAXIMIZING ALL 5 GAUGES

HOW DO PEOPLE ACHIEVE THEIR LIFE SUCCESS DESTINATION?

"So, I grow up to be a loser?"

The Kid | Disney Movies   Bruce Willis THE KID

Instagram credit

One of my all-time favorite movies is "The Kid".

It's a great example of how important it is to have ALL 5 Stars to reach your Life Success Destination.

Bruce Willis plays Russ, a wealthy Los Angeles image consultant to business people, politicians, and stars. He's about to turn 40 and he's become a cynical guy, estranged from his father, and has lost his childhood memories.

One night, a kid named Rusty (brilliantly played by Spencer Beslin) who is about to turn 8 suddenly appears in Russ' lavish, but dark, sad house. Russ mistreats everybody he comes into contact with, including Rusty.

Eventually they figure out they are the same person, that Rusty is Russ as an 8 year old. They have to figure out why he is there so they can go back to their lives.

The famous lines in the movie come from Rusty who looks at Russ (being his future self), and is trying to figure out if he is happy about how his life turns out. At one point Rusty says: "So l am a chick-less, dog-less guy and I don't fly jets" (the kid really wants to be a pilot and have a dog named Chester). When Rusty asks Russ what he does for a living, he tells him what he does as an image consultant and how he makes a lot of money. Rusty, not impressed by the money, sums up the professional explanation as: "So basically you teach people how to lie about who they really are."

I may not have the conversation word for word, but I think his big summary is: "So at 40 I'm not married, I don't even have a girlfriend, I don't have a dog, and I'm not a pilot. **So I grow up to be a loser?**"

That of course sets up the movie to figure out why Russ is basically unhappy and has to change.

I score Russ high on the MONEY Gauge and good on the TALENT Gauge, but not the other three.

I chose to write about this character because I have known so many Russ's. They think they are successful. But other people can't stand them. They hate working for people who have done whatever it takes to get to their own success, and step on people all around them. That's what Russ does.

He gets a 0 on the RELATIONSHIP Gauge.

His OUTLOOK is strong, but only in his own self-interest.

He gets a 10 on the MONEY Gauge. You see his beautiful home and car.

I'd give him a 7 or 8 on the TALENT Gauge. His talents are very strong, but he has no intention of using them to genuinely help others.

He completely flunks the TIME Gauge. He spends all of his time at work and traveling for work and has nothing else.

Which gets me to the last Star, the RELATIONSHIP Gauge. He gets a 0 on it as well. He has no positive relationships. Not one. He's mean to his secretary, his clients, and pretty much every person he comes into contact with.

Overall, Russ' problem is he doesn't even know what Life Success is. That's why he's so unhappy. But he doesn't know it until his younger self reminds him of what he really wanted to be.

See the movie. The end is a tear jerker as well as really fun and motivating! And by now you've guessed that Russ does figure out how to get to his Life Success Destination.

Instagram credit

If you could talk to your 8-year-old self, what advice would you give to yourself?

People who achieve Life Success *know* what they *want* and *go after it*.

Only you can define your own Life Success.

Life Success most always comes through:

Achievements through your work or volunteer life.

1. Feeling that you are maximizing the use of all the talents and expertise that you have.
2. Knowing that you have attained what is important to you.
3. Living life on your own terms.
4. Making sure those you care about are well taken care of.
5. Happiness and contentment with your life and beliefs.

Look at your life. How do you feel about your Life Success Score? Are you closer to your dream work this year than you were last year? Are you:

- Moving forward?

- Falling behind?

- Standing still?

If you are waiting for the perfect time to move forward, I'm pretty sure it won't be happening. **There are** *only two real answers* **to** where you are right now:

1. I am currently doing what I was meant to do....or,

2. I am not.

If it's time to start driving your life forward, how do you get moving? **USE ALL YOUR MAP ANSWERS TO BEGIN TO INCREASE YOUR LIFE SUCCESS SCORE.**
Once you know what you are going to do, you can look at yourself in the mirror and be proud that you are on your way to becoming yourself. You were made you to be happy and successful!

DESIGN YOUR MAP

THE MORE STARS YOU HAVE IN YOUR LIFE SUCCESS GUAGES - THE HAPPIER YOU WILL BE

If you only have a few stars, you won't have full Life Success.

People who reach their Life Success Destination get a lot of other things with it along the way.

TAKE YOUR FAMILY WITH YOU TO YOUR LIFE SUCCESS DESTINATION!

Benefits of Life Success

Getting to your Life Success Destination is definitely not an overnight trip. It's months, maybe years to get there. The benefits of putting in the work to get there are substantial and worth the effort.

SELF WORTH

Every life is significant. You are meant to live a life of significance. Attaining the Life Success Destination you want to have will definitely give you a strong feeling of self-worth and satisfaction. When you work hard for something and you get it, it's a feeling like no other.

It doesn't matter what your title is when you start, or when your reach your Destination. Your self-worth comes from within. I think we are innately wired to either be proud of or be disappointed in how we live our lives. More accomplishments alone won't do it.

That's why I use my 5 Gauges because to get to the highest star Destination you work on all 5. Note none of them have to do with fame or fortune. Self-worth is contentment and pride. You give it to yourself.

GET THE HIGHEST LIFE SUCCESS SCORE YOU CAN GET!!!

CONTROL

In order to reach your goals, along the way you will have gained control of your life. You will also likely have gained a new sense of freedom that you never had before. It's a lifetime of freedom as long as you stay in your Destination. You will be subject to a lot less rules and what other people want from you which will give you freedom to do what you always wanted.

I used to be so jealous of my husband Jack who mostly worked from home. My day was scheduled from 5 am to 7 pm five days a week and I had little control over it.

As much as I wanted more control over the decisions in each company I worked for, at the end of the day all I could do was try my best to influence. There's always a boss making all the final decisions. I never got used to that. I never liked it.

I love having my own work, my own business. I get to make all the decisions. Who I work with, when I work, where I work, what I work on and how I do it. It's amazingly fulfilling. If something isn't going well, I only have myself to blame.

It is possible to get more control while you are an employee, but it will take a strong agreement about expectations for some freedoms.

RESPONSIBILITY

To achieve your Destination, you will have had to take all of the responsibility for getting there. When you operate in the realm of Life Success, you continue to grow and take responsibility for your own life and and for helping others.

STABILITY

You will have to make many decisions along the road to your Destination. Many of those decisions will involve some level of risk. For instance, to stay in your job or to leave for another. To leave to start your own business, or to come up with your own plan for independence. You can make those decisions slowly while maintaining your current stability.

INDEPENDENCE

My experience with helping people to achieve their Life Success is that those who achieve the most success are the ones who desire independence the most. Most often, people who have learned the skills and attitudes of

entrepreneurship feel like they achieve their Life Success. Both employees of organizations, and independent business people all get more Life Success if they understand and use entrepreneurial talents.

The overall end goal will get you not only the Life Success you want, but also the long-term stability to keep going.

When I was the head of Executive Recruiting and Development for a couple of different companies, I was responsible for filling all corporate executive positions, world-wide. I had to find candidates, assess them, and then have the appropriate people interview them. I had the sole responsibility of making the decision over all for executive hires and promotions. Why did they give that to me? Because in all my years of doing it, not one person I hired was ever fired. Some left on their own volition, but no one I hired was ever fired. I managed the top 1000 jobs in each of those companies who had close to 100,000 employees. I hired the smartest and best leaders.

That's why selection is so very important. Putting the right talents into the right job and organization.

But I have a secret to tell. I never once hired anyone I thought would likely come in just to learn from the company for a while, and then leave. For me to be successful in hiring people who would do well for the company, I purposely did not hire anyone who would be too independent. Rogue. In other words, I was not looking for people who would come in and be non-conformist. That's the first thing that will get someone in trouble.

I was also not looking for people who would come in and steal valuable company secrets and then take off to do their own thing to compete with us. It's a fine line distinction to discern who will be a good and decisive leader but will stay loyal to the organization. And we did have many high level people who were not loyal, but no one I ever hired.

So how does this apply to you? If you have that Independent streak in you, go for it on your own. You'll be much happier than confined in an organization you can't control.

Independence has the additional benefits of:
- Removing the the stress of competition with peers at work
- Removing the stress of having to move up the ladder

SECURITY

Everyone reading this book will have experienced the floor dropping out from under them at some point in their lives. I know I have, many times.

I love to remind people "A job is always temporary". There is no such thing as a "permanent employee" because if one day you cross the wrong person or you're late, or they don't need what you do anymore, you're gone.

If you have an option with security it makes it all right. If you don't, it can be very scary. Financial security, having a nice place to live that is paid off, not having a lot of debt, knowing you have that Life Success Insurance Policy you wanted to start with. I think that kind of security is a much better way to live.

Working as an employee or for yourself? Either way it's nice to know you have the security to choose which way to go when you want to.

FAMILY'S WELL-BEING

Long term stability and security are the foundation for happy homes and for raising children who don't have to worry about their parents being stressed about where their lives are going. Will they have what they need to succeed in their own lives?

I firmly believe that achieving your Life Success Destination sets you up as their role model for achieving theirs as well.

Learning how and living your Life Success will not only transform your own life but will affect generations to come. What you teach/role model now for your family (and anyone you mentor) will impact their future.

NO LOOKING IN THE REAR VIEW MIRROR!

You can start where you are and move forward from there, no matter where you are in your life. No sense looking back. That's not where you are headed! STAY OUT OF REVERSE GEAR.

JUST TELL YOURSELF:

I CAN **DO** ANYTHING

I **AM** AWESOME

I CAN **BE** WHAT I WANT TO **BE**

I CAN **HAVE** ANYTHING I WANT.

I **AM** AMAZING

I **AM** TALENTED

I **AM** FULL OF POTENTIAL AND POSSIBILITY

I HAVE **NO** LIMITS

I **DESERVE** A 5 STAR LIFE SUCCESS

HAPPINESS

HAPPINESS: This is one of the **biggest benefits** of all .

WHY ARE SO MANY PEOPLE UNHAPPY AND DISSATISFIED WITH THEIR LIVES?

Have you seen any information, at all, that shows people are getting happier? By all accounts we have researched, happiness is on a downward spiral. Cases of depression have ballooned by 20% in less than a decade and is now the leading cause of disability worldwide. The WHO (World Health Organization) reported there are 300 million+ people worldwide who have depression. A large percentage turn to drugs to reduce the pain of not feeling happy or satisfied with their lives. The results of depression in lost work productivity are $210 billion per year in the US alone!

What I've been emphasizing in this entire book is how to live a Happy Life. If you don't know what makes you happy, you won't get there.

I firmly believe a major contributor is focusing on we don't have instead of what we do have. Being trapped in an unfilled life. Not achieving the dreams we are meant to live.

Look at your life.

Are you happier this year than you were last year?

Are you more successful this year than you were last year?

Are you:

- Moving closer?

- Getting worse?

- Staying the same?

If you are waiting for the perfect time to make changes, it won't be happening. Now is the time. There is no perfect time.

THERE ARE *ONLY TWO REAL ANSWERS* TO WHERE YOU ARE RIGHT NOW:

I AM CURRENTLY HAPPY *OR* I AM NOT

"Everything is in your mind". Ever heard that? It's true. What you perceive is based on how you see your life. And that is based on what we call "Choosing the Channel". Whatever you watch, whatever you perceive you are experiencing, will determine your outcomes.

It is so important it is to release your view of yourself in the past. To reach Life Success requires breathing in the future. Certainly retain the best of the past, but to create a future you need a different view.

Your mind sets your beliefs, emotions and habits which directly affect your relationships and success.

Your mind sets up your dreams. Only your mind sets up the constraints you see in your life. How do you break out of that situation?

It's a matter of getting away from the bad channels you have been watching, experiencing, and stuck in.

Bad channels create a "Life Loop". Have you ever seen a marketing program that sets up a video that just keeps looping over and over again at a store booth?

That's what happens when you get stuck on the wrong Channels, you can't get out of the loop. Existing expectations, responsibilities, conflicts.

But if you continue to watch those channels, get stuck in that life loop, you won't have a clear path to the life of your dreams.

You are wasting time. AND YOU CAN'T GAIN BACK LOST TIME.

You are wasting time that could be progress to get you to Happiness.

Do you think about "What if?" Each day you are stuck on your bad channels focus is a day you can't move forward to happiness. You stay stuck in regret, inaction, depleting your chances.

Your breakthrough will only occur when you "Change the Channel". GO TO LIFE SUCCESS CHANNEL!

It *is important* to determine *what it will take to get to happiness???*

1. Do you think about your own happiness? Why are you happy or unhappy?
   - _____
   -
   - _____
   -
   - _____

What needs to change for me to be happier?

- _____
- _____
- _____
- _____
- _____
- _____

What exactly could make you happier?

- _____
- _____
- _____
- _____
- _____

It is possible to stay in your current job/situation and focus on changing your happiness. Once you understand what is affecting it, you can work on changing that.

There is *something else, something more* that you can do with your life. You have probably felt that. If, just if, *you could find a way to change your life to what you know it could and should be!*

Whatever difficulties or obstructions we may face, we have the power, our own personal power, within ourselves to create our own happiness.

Those who wait for opportunities to come to change their lives may wait until it's too late to have an impact. God gives us the strength and perseverance to break through barriers, to look for and create our own happiness and success. WE CAN AND SHOULD DO THIS FOR OURSELVES.

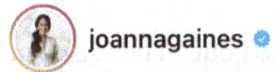
joannagaines

Chip and Joanna Gaines

You've read many stories in this book about people I have worked with. But I wanted to make the last stories about people you know about. People you may have followed in their story attaining Life Success. So I chose to write this last story about Chip and JoAnna Gaines.

You probably know who they are. I could have just said "Chip and Jo" and you would know who I'm talking about. They have an incredible story. I have not met them personally, but our son who graduated from Baylor University in Waco, TX has met them several times at church and says they are very down to earth genuinely nice people.

In 2013 they launched their HGTV show "Fixer Upper" which is about home remodeling in their famous farm chic design.

Chip started multiple businesses even while he was going to Baylor. His first substantial business was in home construction. They about went broke on one huge investment he made, but it all worked out. They still operate Magnolia Homes, a design, construction and Magnolia Realty real estate company. One thing they have done their entire married life is take a lot of risks.

That risk taking has led them to build many substantial businesses: Magnolia Market at the Silos which is several blocks of stores, a church, Magnolia Table Restaurant, luxury B & B's, their own line of furniture, their own line of home goods with Target, their magazine Magnolia Journal, and they published several books. Along the way, they had five children while having the most popular show on HGTV.

"Jo and I had multiple opportunities to quit and it's just not in our DNA. Jo and I are not quitters. Throwing in the towel is just not something that ever comes to mind", he was quoted in an interview. He has a totally positive OUTLOOK!

They did five extremely popular seasons of "Fixer Upper" and became the model for over 50 other shows that have tried to copy their success doing home makeovers.

After all that, they took a break from HGTV to plan their own TV Network, Magnolia Network with all their own shows. They bought the Discovery DIY Network and built all new shows. They accomplished that during the year and a half where most TV stations stopped filming because of COVID. They still got it done.

Here's my review of the 5 Gauges and the LIFE SUCCESS SCORE for Chip and Jo.

TIME: No matter how much Chip and Jo have going on, they always prioritize time with their family. They have always had the children involved in whatever they do. The kids were in every TV episode and Chip and Jo made it clear that the kids were their number one priority. They also involved their parents and community members in everything they did.

I think that's what made it possible to do everything they were able to accomplish. It all got rolled into one.

TALENTS: It's clear they both use their natural talents to the fullest. And they have a really good talent for finding people with incredible business and creative talents. In their blogs, they always show who's working with them. Staff and community. That's the key to talents is to find out what you have, what you need, and to fill in the gaps by yourself or from others. Their biggest talent is knowing what to do next.

MONEY: They admit they came close to losing everything they had a few different times. Neither came from money so they only had themselves to rely on. I can't find any realistic estimate of what they are worth. From my business experience it looks like they control hundreds of millions of dollars worth of assets. And they have done all that in about 15 years.

They still live in the rural farm home they bought early in their marriage. They have remodeled it, and it's beautiful, but nothing extraordinary. What is extraordinary is the farm they built. Beautiful gardens, and tons of animals. Chip has a big heart for whoever needs a home. And he has shown his children how to love people and animals in need.

I think their view of money is that it was never their priority. It was always about building something of value for other people. Everything they have done is based on a product or service helping people at all income levels. I believe they are very generous givers in their community and have done a lot of projects giving their own time and materials.

Money comes to people in different ways. They have worked really hard, but they sure made it look easy.

OUTLOOK: I've seen Jo and Chip change over the years. He was the funny one and she was the introverted shy one. As their businesses have grown I've noticed their public personalities have also matured. Having to run so many businesses would require a lot of seriousness, but they still make it look fun.

Their overall OUTLOOK has never changed: Get the vision and run with it. And don't give up until you achieve your goal. I can't think of any other couple, working together in the same business, who has accomplished what they have in such a short time. I believe their OUTLOOK is responsible for a lot of it.

RELATIONSHIPS: They are known in Waco as the couple who has put Waco on the map. Building bridges from the high and the low sides of town. They are famous for investing in dilapidated old areas and bringing them back to life. People love them.

I give them a 5 Star Life Success Destination. They get it because they involved so many people along to way. Helping them. Then those people helped to make Chip and Jo extremely successful in all they do.

So many people don't make time to build Life Success. They always made the time.

Do I expect you to be a Chip and Jo example of Life Success?

Only if you want to be!

In the end, it's your Life Success Destination and you are the one who will decide what and where it is.

When people see Chip and Jo they see their success.

What they don't see is what it took to get there.

Another iceberg analogy:

Chip and Jo have written about how much they had to learn, how hard the work is. They never gave up and had to sacrifice a lot. But with discipline and dedication they achieved their Life Success.

THEY GET 5 STARS AND 50 POINTS

LIFE SUCCESS SCORE!!!!!

YOUR GAUGES ALL IMPACT EACH OTHER

Just like a car works, all 5 of your Gauges need to work well *at the same time* in order to maximize your Life Success.

Many movies you'll see work on this same premise. A person is in dire straights because some part of their life isn't working. I saw a movie last night where a young woman could not hold down a job, or make any money, because she didn't perceive that she had any talents. (She was dyslexic which made it worse). Such a mess no one in her family would let her live with them (no good Relationships). She was a menace to herself and others. She could not manage her own Time.

She went to live with her grandmother in a retirement community and grandma got her a job taking care of people. That turned her life around. She made friends (Relationships), found she had a lot of talents to use and turned those into a business with grandma's help. Making lots of Money, feeling good about herself (Outlook) and grandma helped with managing her Time to start. All her Relationships are mended and she lives happily ever after. A formula for Life Success!

When one gauge is way too low, it definitely impacts all of the others.

Once you know the 5 Gauges of Life Success, you will see how they influence everyone's story.

SO NOW WHAT?

Now that you know all this, how will you use this incredible power to move forward?

BECAUSE YOU DO HAVE TO MAKE CHOICES. YOU DO HAVE TO MAKE DECISIONS. If you make the right decisions, people will give you money for your products or services.

HOW WILL CHOOSE TO LIVE YOUR LIFE SUCCESS?

WHAT IS THE BIGGEST CHALLENGE YOU HAVE NOW? WHICH GAUGES NEED TO BE FILLED UP FIRST TO OVERCOME THAT CHALLENGE?

Is your time spent attaining others' goals, being dependent on their dreams, or do you spend your time building your own goals and independence?

The rest of your life starts NOW! Do you know what you want to do with the rest of your life?

EXCUSES

It is necessary to move beyond the boundaries that others set for us. Far too often peer pressures and economic dependency are used as excuses for not being happy. Don't choose to stay in those prisons. Your happiness depends on you, not anyone else.

Make your own Happiness!

START YOUR ENGINE WITH

THE LIFE SUCCESS ACTION PLAN

When it's time to start driving your life forward, what do you have to do to get moving? PLAN TO ACHIEVE YOUR LIFE SUCCESS.

Life Success Coaching is a great way to get moving quickly! My coaching program includes the companion book to this: *The Life Success Action Plan.* You can work with me step by step using the MAP you have built with your own answers *and much more* to improve your 5 Gauges Life Success Score to get you to your Life Success Destination. *We can work together to design your new career or to start an independent business.*
You will make fast progress working with someone who can help you all along the way.

What is your Life Success Dream?

Life Success Dreams Inspire Big Changes!

HAVE YOU ARRIVED AT *YOUR*

LIFE SUCCESS DESTINATION?

PROGRESS CHECKPOINTS

You won't encounter *any* speed limit signs along the road to your Life Success. You can go as fast as you want to.

Whenever you feel like you're making progress, re-take the Life Success Assessment to see if you've gotten enough Yes scores to gain another star!

A FINAL NOTE

I am so grateful for the experience gained in my own career. I have had a birds-eye view of thousands and thousands of people in their careers and learned from managing them. I also learned from my own career mistakes. I saw how corporate decisions impacted the individuals within the organization; sometimes positively, many times not. There are some good, well-meaning organizations out there where employees can be happy and fulfilled in their careers. However, my experience, and most studies provide unquestionable evidence that most of the working population are not happy and fulfilled in their current environments.

Many people dream about having their own business. Many who are unemployed who want to have successful, meaningful life and career opportunities. It is clear they want to change their lives but don't know how to do it.

When I left the corporate world and went out on my own (with Jack, my husband and business partner), it was the most freeing experience I'd ever had. We were so fortunate that our first executive recruiting client company provided us with enough work that it completely replaced my corporate income. It certainly hasn't always been like that.

Being consultants allowed us the freedom to do what we thought was best for our clients, our candidates, and the people we coached. When we found the company was not going to be right, we would pull the candidates. When we determined the company was not ethical or treated employees unfairly, we fired the company.

For the time we've been on our own we have been completely dedicated to serving our individual clients needing help with their careers. People who know they want more but don't know how to get there.

I have been so blessed to help people who I can truly say are happier now than they were before I worked with them. I helped them realize what they could really do with their careers and their lives. And that makes me happy.

Each individual Life Success Destination requires personalized directions to get there. I design a personal Life Success Action Plan for each of our clients. That's what I love to do, make a specific MAP for each person and we work it together.

If you are interested in working together on your Life Success Action Plan, please contact me:

Deborah@LifeSuccessChannel.com

Deborah and Jack Gentry

Call for your

Reservation!

423 602 2669